LONDON TO CALCUTTA 1938

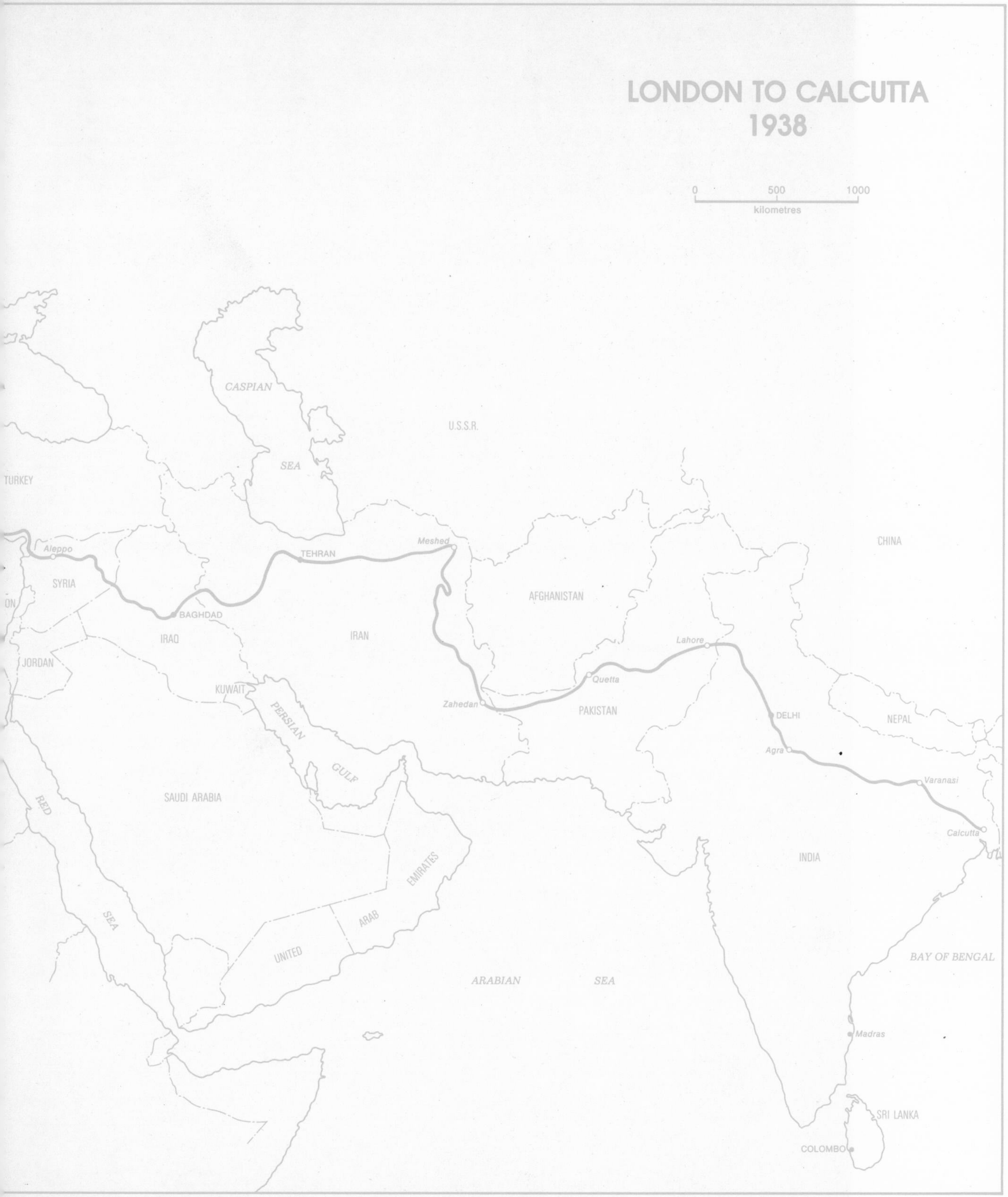

LONDON TO CALCUTTA
1938

EDITORIAL NOTE regarding the Maps.

For ease of understanding we have chosen to use the current political boundaries of the countries through which Owen Wright and Ted White passed.

Little Hills Press Pty. Ltd.,
Tavistock House,
34 Bromham Road,
Bedford. MK40 2QD
United Kingdom

Regent House,
37-43 Alexander St.,
Crows Nest NSW 2065
Australia

Designed by Michelle Havenstein
Production by Vantage Graphics
Printed in Singapore by Kyodo-Shing Loong Pty Ltd.,

ISBN 0 949773 80 8

National Library of Australia
Cataloguing-in-Publication data.

Wright, Owen, 1913—
London to Calcutta 1938.

ISBN 0 949773 80 8.

1. Wright, Owen, 1913— — Journeys.
2. White, E.L.D., 1906— — Journeys.
3. Voyages and travels. 4. Europe — Description
and travel — 1919-1944. 5. Turkey — Description
and travel. 6. Iran — Description and travel.
I. White, E.L.D., 1906 — . II. Title.

910.4

LONDON TO CALCUTTA
1938

O.D. WRIGHT and E.L.D. WHITE

LITTLE HILLS PRESS

Camel caravan on the road down to the Indus Plain.

CONTENTS

Late afternoon shadows across a street in Tarsus, Turkey.

PREFACE

In the latter part of 1938, my cousin Ted White and I decided to drive Ted's old Morris car from London to Calcutta.

Lightly built and not very tall, with a philosophical outlook on life and a sense of humour, Ted was to make a good companion on a long and uncomfortable trip. Then thirty-one, he was by profession an engineer and had been working at Croydon in South London for two years with a firm that specialised in designing and building electrical equipment for unusual purposes (such as an instrument that showed the helmsman the position of the weathercock on the top of the mast of Sir Thomas Lipton's yacht *Shamrock*, one of his several unsuccessful contenders for the America's Cup). Part of Ted's education had been in England, and his experience of the world was much greater than mine. He also possessed university degrees in Science and Engineering and so had a professional's regard for accuracy and detail, which was to stand him in good stead in his later wartime job as Assistant Secretary (research) in the Australian Defence Department.

I was twenty-five and had arrived in England in March of that year without any definite program in mind except to see as much of the Old World as I could, with the limited time and money that I had available. Unlike Ted, I had spent most of my life on my father's property on the New England Tableland in northern New South Wales among sheep and cattle. I did, however, have a bias towards mechanical things and an interest in motor cars that was soon to be given greater development. I was taller than Ted, but just as lightly built, and temperamentally we had a lot in common, which no doubt helped us to get along together through nearly three months of close proximity, with only occasional differences that did not stay with us for long.

We used to spend time together whenever I was in London and we were both due to leave Britain and go home to Australia before the end of the year. So instead of spending five or six weeks and the price of the ticket on the voyage home, we decided to travel overland together as far as it was feasible to go.

Enquiries soon showed us that the furthest point that we could hope to reach, without shipping our car a long distance, would be Calcutta. There was, we learned, at that time no way of getting into Burma from the west through the dense jungles and rushing rivers of the Chin Hills, in the hope of then going south down the Irawaddy River to Mandalay and eventually picking up a ship sailing to Australia from Rangoon.

JULY, 1938.

Wednesday 13

I spent most of the day making inquiries about the possibility of making a car trip to India with Ted.
Saw the R.A.C. & then went to the Editor of the Autocar who gave me some help & a letter to the head of the Foreign Touring dept of the A.A.
Watched Queen Mary go down the river to the Tower.
Had lunch with Lena Archie Lindel came up to town this evening & he, Peter, Lena & I had dinner & then Archie, Ted & I went to the Pictures

An entry from Owen's diary for Wednesday, 13 July 1938.

In fact, it was not until after the invasion of Burma by the Japanese during the Second World War that overland communications with India were developed, even to their present limited extent, as part of a strategy to counter the imminent threat to the 'Jewel in the Crown'.

We kept a simple logbook during our trip, in which we carefully entered places, times and distances. In the early stages this may have seemed to be a rather pointless exercise, but as we went further east and the signposts became fewer and less comprehensible, we were to find ourselves depending more and more on the logbook as a record of where we had been and at what time. A check back on elapsed times and speedometer readings was often our only way of placing our position on a map.

Besides the logbook, to which we both contributed, I kept a brief diary. Both of these have survived the years and, along with a few other written records and a lot of photographs, have proved to be great stimulants for our otherwise fading memories.

Ted was the chief photographer and the proud owner of a new Leica, then the world's best camera, with quite a lot of flexibility but without any of the array of different lenses that people carry now. I had a faithful old bellows-type Voigtlander with a 4.5 lens. Colour film was then relatively uncommon and probably nowhere near as reliable as it is now and, since neither of us had had any experience with it, we decided not to take any along; a good decision, as the results would not have lasted through the years in the way that the black and white prints and films have done.

That it has taken so many years to set this story down is mainly due to the changes to our lives that happened after Ted and I made our different ways home from Calcutta at the end of 1938. Our respective marriages and the outbreak of the Second World War and the events that followed combined to keep us living separate and busy lives in different states, a thousand miles apart, with only occasional meetings.

Consequently, it was not long ago that we decided that something should be done to make use of the photographs and written records that were still available about the journey that, though uneventful in itself, took place half a century ago, in a world that has undergone huge changes since those days.

This book is the result of that decision.

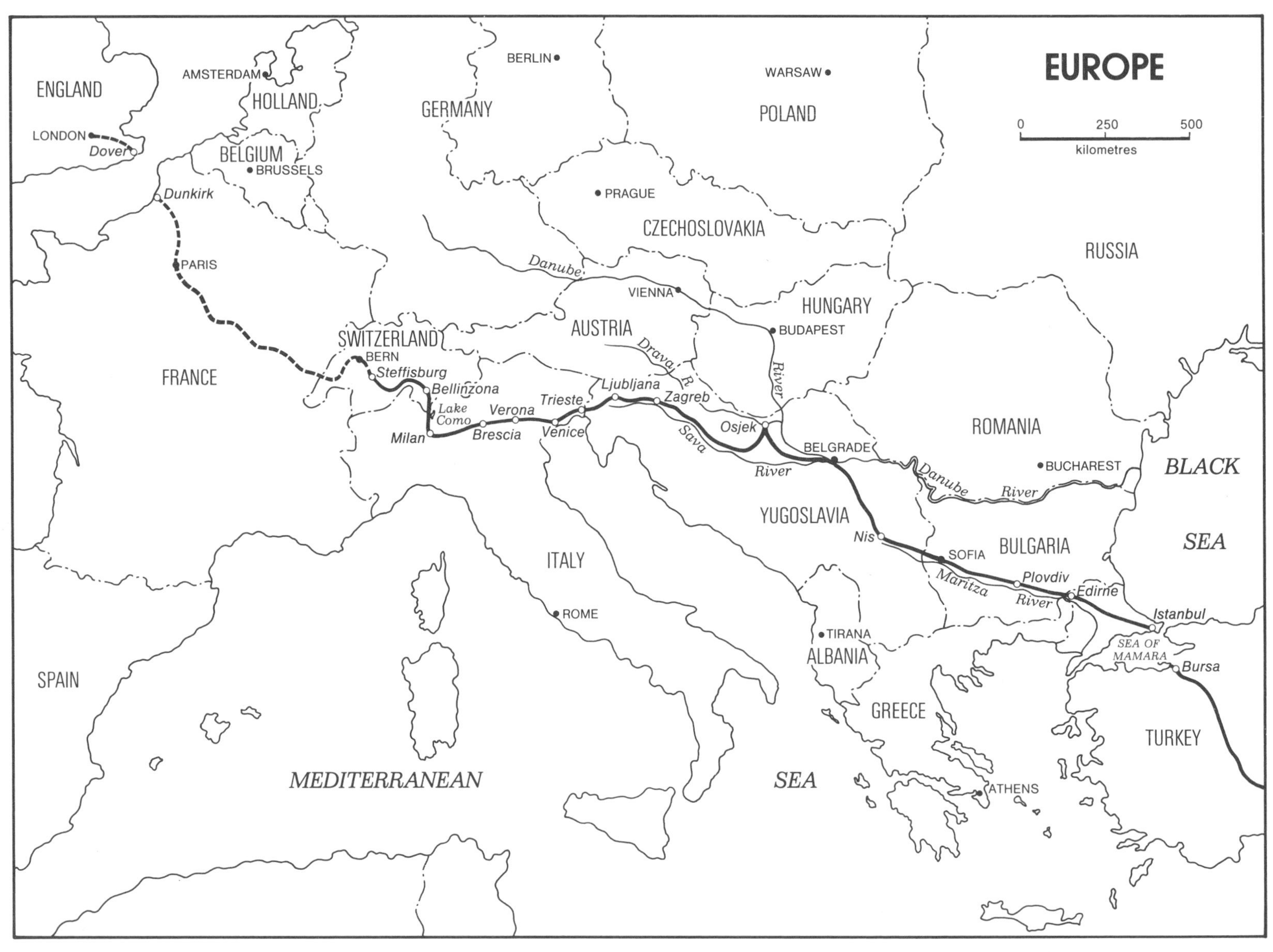
EUROPE
0
250
500
kilometres
ENGLAND
LONDON
Dover
AMSTERDAM
HOLLAND
BELGIUM
BRUSSELS
Dunkirk
PARIS
FRANCE
GERMANY
BERLIN
POLAND
WARSAW
PRAGUE
CZECHOSLOVAKIA
RUSSIA
Danube
VIENNA
AUSTRIA
HUNGARY
BUDAPEST
SWITZERLAND
BERN
Steffisburg
Bellinzona
Lake Como
Milan
Verona
Brescia
Trieste
Venice
Ljubljana
Zagreb
Drava R.
River
Sava
Osjek
River
BELGRADE
ROMANIA
BUCHAREST
Danube
River
BLACK
SEA
YUGOSLAVIA
Nis
SOFIA
BULGARIA
Plovdiv
Maritza
River
Edirne
Istanbul
SEA OF MAMARA
Bursa
TURKEY
ITALY
ROME
TIRANA
ALBANIA
GREECE
ATHENS
SPAIN
MEDITERRANEAN
SEA

1

EUROPE

'Altogether it is a marvellous idea and we are very keen on it, but I do hope that you and Dad won't think it too hare-brained . . . ' So I wrote to my parents from London on 3 August 1938.

Ted and I had then only vague ideas about the actual route we should take, but the more we thought about the trip and discussed it with friends, the less difficult it seemed to be; the journey apparently being done occasionally by army officers going to and from India. While there were some hazards, both political and practical, it seemed likely that these could be overcome, or at least avoided.

In this, the year before the Second World War actually began, the peoples of Europe stood in considerable fear of what Adolf Hitler and the Germans might do next.

During the four years since he had become Chancellor of Germany, Hitler had re-occupied the Ruhr and the Saar valleys, industrial areas of Germany occupied by the Allies under the Treaty of Versailles, and had then seized the Republic of Austria, on the excuse that its people were in fact of German blood. Now he was threatening to treat Czecho-Slovakia in the same brutal fashion, using as an excuse his alleged concern for the well-being of the Sudeten German minority in that country, and again declaring, as he had on previous occasions, that this would be the last of his territorial ambitions in Europe.

In spite of the obvious dangers of this situation, the countries which did not clearly stand in his path continued to maintain an uneasy peace with their neighbours; intent on preserving the illusion that things would return to 'normal', once Hitler had expanded the borders of his Third Reich to include all those nations or peoples that could possibly be described as being part of the Germanic World.

Outside Europe there was constant unrest in the 'Near East', as the Jews sporadically fought the British, who were trying to limit their movement from Europe, because of the threat of Nazi oppression, to the 'Promised Land' of Israel; the area of which they then sought to expand at the expense of the Palestinian Arabs. The Arabs in their turn also attacked the British, who were the holders of the League of Nations Mandate over Palestine, after the defeat of the Turks at the end of the First World War, blaming them for not preventing the settlement of the Jews on Arab lands; so that Britain had to bear the blame and endure armed rebellion, from both sides.

The name 'Palestine' described an area which roughly included what are now Israel and Jordan along with Lebanon and part of Syria; all of which had been under the rule of the old Turkish Ottoman Empire.

After years of bitter warfare, Palestine had fallen to the Allies in 1918, when the Turks were gradually driven northward towards their homeland by General Allenby's victorious army, aided by the Arabs under Colonel T.E. Lawrence; in which operations the Australian Light Horse, in what was called the 'Desert Mounted Corps', had played an important part.

Further east the Iranians were reputed to be difficult in their attitude to foreign travellers, but it was also said that they traditionally feared and hated the Russians most of all, and that British subjects (as of course we were) would have no great difficulty in obtaining freedom of passage through their country.

Gradually the outline of our proposed route became clearer to us.

Across Europe we had various options, but it seemed that all of them would lead us to Istanbul. We must then traverse Anatolia ('Turkey in Asia') from north to south and enter Syria, proceeding further south at least as far as Aleppo, where we could either turn east to the Euphrates River and follow it south-east down to Baghdad, or else keep a southerly course for about another 200 miles, as far as Damascus. From there a track went east straight across the Syrian Desert for some 400 miles to join the road that ran down the river at Ramadi, not far west of Baghdad. It seemed obvious that a decision on this last choice would best be left until we were close enough to assess the prevailing political situation in Palestine, which could not be predicted far ahead.

After Baghdad we would turn north-east into the mountains of Iran and follow what appeared on the map to be the only practicable road up to the capital, Teheran, and thence to go east again across the Iranian Plateau to Meshed, near the far northern 'corner' of the country, close to where the Russian and Afghan borders joined it.

Then the choice seemed to lie between travelling either south-east through Afghanistan by way of Herat and Kabul and so into India by the Khyber Pass, or else directly south, skirting Afghan territory, to enter British Baluchistan (now the western province of Pakistan) about 400 miles to the west of the town of Quetta. This decision might also depend on future advice about political and other conditions.

We felt rather daunted by the prospect of tackling this particular section of the journey, because of its remoteness from European influence. But at least we were confident, such was our faith in the power of the British Raj, that once we had entered India, even though we might still be nearly 2000 road miles from Calcutta, we would come under its protection and that consequently most of our troubles would be over.

Having thus worked out a rough outline of the way we should go, our next problem was to decide what kind of vehicle to use for the journey. This was before the days of the now ubiquitous four-wheel-drive and, though Land Rovers may have been under development for the British Army about that time, they were not yet known to the public, while if the Americans had already invented the Jeep, it too was still a kind of 'military secret'. Some heavy army trucks drove on all four wheels, but no light commercial types were available in the market and of course no one then thought of four-wheel-drive as being necessary, or even desirable, for any kind of normal travel.

In any case the question was largely an academic one, since we certainly could not

Owen on the outskirts of a village in Yugoslavia, preparing to camp for the night.

have afforded to buy such a vehicle, even if one had been available, and so it did not take us long to decide that Ted's old Morris would have to do the job.

He had owned this already venerable-looking motor car since he had come to England, having bought it in 1936 for fifty-one pounds sterling from his father's brother Alfred, who farmed at Ardley, not far from Oxford. It was a 14/32 model Morris Cowley four-door sedan, made in 1931 and of a type not often seen in Australia, being one of the first of the marque to be produced with a flat-fronted radiator, as distinct from the older 'bull-nosed' variety.

The engine was a very basic four-cylinder side valve design, rated at 13.9 horse power under the old Royal Automobile Club system of calculation, based mainly on engine capacity, which in this case was 1.8 litres. The gear-box was a three speed 'crash' type, having no syncro-mesh to help the driver to change gears smoothly, and there were semi-elliptic leaf springs fitted front and rear. But we did have the then modern innovation of hydraulic brakes on all four wheels. The body colour was a sombre dark brown, and the mudguards were finished in shiny black.

Though it had some obvious shortcomings as a vehicle in which to undertake what was then a long hard journey over bad roads, and with a heavy load, the Morris did have certain features that made it adaptable for the kind of conditions that we expected to meet once we had left the relatively well-made roads and adequate repair shops of Europe behind us.

The first of these concerned the ignition. The car was fitted with what had by then become the standard coil and distributor system, but earlier productions of the same engine had used a magneto instead, and provision for mounting and driving one was still carried on this model. Therefore it was a simple matter for us to fit another 'maggy' back into the old position and then at once we had insurance against failure of either the coil or the distributor, or for that matter, of the battery as well.

It was much the same with the fuel system. The existing tank was too small to carry us very far from a petrol bowser, so we fitted another much larger one, bought from the wreckers, on to the back of the car (there was no boot) and further supplemented the storage with a third and smaller tank under the bonnet. This last could then be used to provide a gravity feed to the carburettor in an emergency, such as would occur if the fuel pump failed. That never happened, but the ignition did in fact pack-up only three days out of England and Ted then re-connected the magneto, which functioned reliably for the rest of the trip.

At the same time as these alterations were being made at a garage in Croydon, near where he lived, Ted decided that the engine should also have a complete overhaul, including re-boring the cylinders and fitting new pistons, rings and bearings, as well as a water pump in place of the old thermo-siphon system. All this put an extra twenty pounds sterling onto the total cost of our preparations, which we could ill-afford, but we had the satistfaction of knowing that when we set out the car would be in good shape mechanically.

Ted had the clever idea of writing to Morris Motors to try to obtain some sort of sponsorship, though nothing was to come of it. However, we had an amusing letter from them when we wrote for information about spare parts. They seemed slightly horrified that we were doing such a trip in such a car but wished us all sorts of luck, while the

Our elegant mobile, parked in the main square of Trieste, in front of the Government Offices.

AUGUST, 1938.

Tuesday 23

Finished packing etc & said good bye to Iris after lunch.
Caught 3 pm train from Victoria to Dover & thence to Ostend. there got train at 9 pm for Munich via Brussels, Cologne & Frankfurt.

AUGUST, 1938.

Wednesday 24

Did not get much sleep last night.
Fine morning with some fog. Reached Frankfurt about 7 am & went on via Wurzburg & Ansbach to Munich at 1.30. Ted & Margot met me. After lunch went to Exhibition of German Art 1938 & saw Nazi memorials & the "Braune Haus".
Went to the Hofbrau Haus this evening.
Stayed Pensione ~~Osb~~ Osborne, Franz Josef Str.

Entries from Owen's diary for 23–24 August 1938.

Publicity Department asked for some photographs of the car in 'equitorial surroundings'. We thought of taking the Morris to Whipsnade Zoo and posing a few monkeys on the roof and sending them that!

For my part I busied myself with buying some fairly basic camping gear, including a tiny petrol-burning primus (we did not want to carry more than one kind of fuel) and a similar type of blow-lamp, a soldering iron and an assortment of other tools, a primitive little ex-army marching compass, a small tent, a couple of canvas stretchers and two very inadequate blanket sleeping bags. It was high summer in England then, and we thought more about the heat of the desert than the cold of the Iranian mountains and suffered accordingly later on, to the extent that we sometimes had to supplement our bedding by sleeping with some scraps of old newspapers under us, in a rather unsuccessful attempt to provide some extra insulation between us and the chill of the Iranian nights.

Because weight was such an important factor for us, we carried no large supply of food, at least in the first stages of the journey, having no doubts that we would do best to live off the land, and of course the same applied to fuel. Apparently this last consideration was not obvious to everyone though, because when we got home I was shown a cutting from a gossip column in a Sydney paper, wherein it was said that we had started out carrying 500 gallons (about 2200 litres) of petrol, which alone would have weighed about two tonnes.

We did assemble quite a comprehensive and heavy box of spare parts that included front and rear springs and a spare differential, but not, unfortunately as it turned out, a spare back axle. We also bought a pair of heavy-treaded tyres (then called 'competition' tyres, because they were used in hill-climbing contests) to be fitted to the back wheels when we came on to unsealed roads, and we had a small drum of water mounted on the running-board, with which we would have to make do for either drinking or washing.

Procuring visas for the countries that we expected to visit and buying the necessary maps to cover our planned route presented no great problems, except that the Iranians would only grant us a transit visa for a period of fourteen days. When we protested that this would not be long enough to allow us to traverse a country as large as Iran, we were assured that in Teheran we would have positively no difficulty in getting whatever extension of time we might desire, a promise that was later to acquire a very hollow ring about it. We also found that the available maps of Iran, and the Middle East generally, were fairly small-scale (1 to 4,000,000 or smaller) and with limited information on them as far as roads were concerned.

Ted was still working at Croydon, so it fell to me to do most of the shopping, which was not a big task; to make the rounds of the consulates and to approach the RAC for whatever information was available about the roads we planned to travel over. The latter were very helpful and even gave us a written report on the road conditions right through to Calcutta, which proved to be reasonably reliable (until we lost it in Istanbul) especially as regards the pessimistic forecasts about what we would have to face once we were beyond the eastern borders of Italy.

By this time it was past the middle of August. We reckoned that we should begin our trip no later than the end of the month, so as to be over the mountain passes near Hamadan that lead on to the Iranian plateau, before there was any risk that we might strike early snow falls there. By now we began to feel a sense of urgency in our preparations. I had booked a passage from Colombo to Sydney in late November and Ted had planned to take a ship from Calcutta to Rangoon at about the same time.

In the meantime our plans were complicated by my wish to go over to Europe, before beginning the trip, for a pre-arranged meeting with two Australian friends Margot and Ted Marriott in Munich, and to spend a while with them, travelling in Bavaria and Switzerland. This left Ted White to make the rest of the final preparations by himself, but he cheerfully agreed to do this so it was arranged that he should travel the first stage with an Austrian friend, George Konreid, and that we should meet in Switzerland at the beginning of September.

The old city, Nuremburg.

During that last week of August, however, an unscheduled event occurred. I became engaged to Margot in Nuremberg, then, in its walled and moated centre at least, still a beautiful mediaeval city, its ancient buildings (now probably bombed out of existence) only partially defaced by the hundreds of red, white and black swastika banners, and the thousands of troops and SS men assembled there for an exercise that demonstrated just how effectively Hitler could use the power of the Nazi propaganda machine to put pressure on visiting statesmen from neighbouring countries.

In this case the visitor was Admiral Horthy, the Regent of Hungary, twin country to Austria, which Hitler had already invaded and declared to be 'united' with Germany by the 'Anschluss'. Horthy had been invited to Berlin for 'talks' with Hitler and was now on his way home to Budapest, accompanied thus far by the Fuehrer's deputy, Rudolph Hess. It was close to the time for the great annual Nuremburg Rally of the Nazi Party, and so no doubt extra men were ready at hand to stage a special event, designed to show to the admiral the strength and unity of the German people.

Overnight the city was filled with thousands of SS men wearing black uniforms and steel helmets and by mid-morning they had lined the route of the procession, now also hung with red, white and green Hungarian flags. By removing the shoulder straps from their belts and linking them together, they formed a continuous barrier between the roadway and the crowd on the footpath, the men facing alternately inwards and outwards.

We already understood by then that it was not altogether prudent for non-Germans to become mixed up in such gatherings, unless they were prepared to risk being abused for not having given the Nazi salute when everyone else was giving it.

This was something we had learnt a few days before while we were in Munich, the Bavarian city about a hundred miles south of Nuremburg, which had been the birthplace of the Nazi Party in the early 1920s. We had spent a couple of days there staying at the Pension Osborne; a boarding-house which I described, in one of my rather infrequent letters to my parents, as being kept by 'a very nice old German lady named Osborne'.

Frau Osborne, in spite of her English name and her fluency in the language, was very much a German and I also described her as being 'a keen Nazi, who had known Hitler and also Hess, his right-hand man, for years'; something which would have given her a distinction that we did not fully appreciate at the time.

In Munich, let into the wall of a building near the centre of the city, was a large tablet commemorating those early members of the NSDAP (National Sozialistsche Deutsche Arbeiter Partei) or in English 'Nazi Party' for short, who had been killed during Hitler's first abortive 'Putsch' for power in 1923. All good Germans gave the Nazi salute and 'Heiled Hitler' as they passed this spot and those foreigners, such as the Marriotts

Rudolf Hess and Admiral Horthy drive past an admiring crowd. Nuremburg, August 1938.

The Lorenz Kirche, Nuremburg, in 1938.

About to depart on the trip: L–R, George Konreid, Ted Marriott, Owen and Margot Marriott.

and myself, who did not wish to do this, took care to pass by on the other side of the street.

And so, in Nuremburg that morning, we settled down at a table beside an upstairs window of a cafe, giving us a good view of the street below, and waited for the show to begin.

The procession did not take long to arrive, and it was over almost as soon as it began. When we were half-way through our coffee, a number of big black open Mercedes staff cars appeared, one behind the other and all travelling at a brisk pace; the crowd 'heiling' and waving paper Hungarian and German swastika flags, provided freely for the occasion, as they swept past. In the back seat of the third car could clearly be seen the brown-shirted figure of Hess and seated beside him someone in a gold-braided naval uniform — evidently Horthy.

I managed a snapshot through the window with my old camera as they went by, and have sometimes wondered since if I should have tossed down a hand-grenade instead.

When the crowds dispersed (as they soon did, for there was nothing else to see and the weather was grey and damp) we drove back, through the other old mediaeval towns of Dinkelsbuhl and Rothenburg-ober-Tauber, to Munich and Frau Osborne's hospitable establishment.

That evening we celebrated the new engagement with a visit to the National Opera House, where we stood in the 'gods' to hear, and by standing on tip-toe and peering forward, to see at least part of a performance of *Lo"hengrin*. After that we adjourned to a nearby 'wein keller' called the Regina Bar, where we drank two bottles of Rheingold champagne and then walked a little unsteadily back to the pension.

All this activity made no real difference to the plans that Ted and I had made for our trip home, and Margot raised no objections, but of course the engagement did provide a very strong reason for me to be back in Australia by, or at least near to, the promised date in early December. There was, I felt, always the risk that she might change her mind.

During the next week our two parties met, according to plan, in the village of Steffisburg, near Thun, chosen because it was the home of a Swiss named Ernst Krahenbuhel, who had emigrated to Australia to become a professional shearer under the pseudonym of 'Ernie Jones' and had shorn at Dyamberin, for several seasons. While on his last visit there, he had stated his intention of returning to Switzerland to see his family and I had agreed to meet him there in his home village, if it could be arranged. He was on hand to greet us when we arrived at Steffisburgh and he installed us all in the Pension Schnittweierbad, a large and comfortable family 'Gasthaus'.

Ernst was a cheerful character and under his guidance we all spent two happy days walking in the foothills of the Jungfrau Range and one afternoon going to Thun to visit a big bull market and show of the yellow and white Swiss cattle, which the locals called Simmentalers.

Finally, on a wet Sunday morning, 4 September, we loaded up the car, took photographs and said goodbyes. I put on my 'solar topee', a cork-lined helmet bought specially for travel in the tropics, and we started up the Morris and set out for India.

It was a very rainy day and fog obscured the views of the Swiss Alps as we drove along the edge of the Thuner See, through Interlaken and Meiringen and over the Furka Pass,

The banner in this street in Rothenburg ober Tauber, near Nuremberg, is a mild indication of what was to come.

Ernst and friend.

The road over the St Gothard Pass snakes around hairpin bends.

Granite poles in a Bellinzonna vineyard, split quite finely and used to support grapevines.

A view from the lofty spires of the Milan Cathedral looking over the city.

and finally down the extraordinary twists and turns of the St Gothard into the more temperate climate of the Italian side of Switzerland, the canton of Ticino.

There the road ran through vineyards growing up the sides of the valley of the Ticino River, the vines supported by 'poles' made from long splinters of granite, difficult to split no doubt, but certainly everlasting.

We reached Bellinzona as night fell at the end of our first day out, having travelled not much over a hundred miles, but feeling as if it had been a good deal further; and lodged for the night in a plain but adequate hotel, aptly named the Casa del Populi.

The following morning was bright and sunny when we left Bellinzona and headed south towards the Italian border, our good spirits somewhat dashed, first by battery trouble, and next by the engine, perhaps not yet quite run-in after its overhaul, running so hot that it almost seized as we climbed out of the valley. It cooled off, however, apparently without doing itself any harm, as we crossed over the range and ran happily down to the shores of Lake Lugano.

We entered Italy at the frontier town of Chiasso, three hours, but less than fifty miles, out of Bellinzona. My main memory of Chiasso is of the good humour of the Italian frontier guards, evidently Bersaglieri, because they wore broad-brimmed felt hats, each decorated with the tail feathers of a black rooster. Perhaps I was surprised, after the heel

La Chiesa di San Giorgio, Venice.

clicking and 'heiling Hitler' of the officials in Germany, that their Italian counterparts showed no signs of any Fascist hostility towards us, in spite of the then close alliance between Hitler and Mussolini.

It might have been their amiability that prompted Ted, as we drove through the gates, to give them all a cheery wave that encompassed nearby Lake Como, shimmering in the sunshine of an autumn morning, and, in their native tongue, to wish them 'Buena vista!'.

We stopped for a short walk on the shores of the lake to admire its beauty and that of the surrounding alps, but soon we were having our first experience of one of Mussolini's new autostradas as we sped into Milan.

We stayed there for only two hours, at first inside the cathedral, but later up on its roof, admiring the intricate stone carvings, the marble statues of the saints on the numerous spires and the maze of flying buttresses that seemed to be all around us.

A heavy thunderstorm broke over us as we left the city and drove east through Bergamo as far as Brescia, arriving after dark and having some difficulty in finding a hotel, which caused us to put up in a rather more expensive place than we would otherwise have chosen. We had planned to camp out as much as we could, but it seemed that nowhere in Switzerland or Northern Italy was there any room along the roads for us to put up our tent, nor was there any provision for organised camping places for tourists, no doubt because in those days the only caravans on the roads were drawn by horses and driven by gipsies, and also because small hotels in the villages were generally clean and very cheap.

Moreover, as we travelled east across the Plain of Lombardy, through those Shakespearean-sounding cities of Verona, Padua and Venice, already driven forward by the feeling that, with so far to go and so many exotic places to be seen outside Europe, we could not afford to stop for long to enjoy the beauties of Northern Italy.

We did permit ourselves an afternoon in Venice (absurd though such an inadequate time might sound) where, in those happy pre-tourism days, St Mark's Square, on a sunny afternoon, was almost bare of people.

That night we stopped in the small town of San Dona' di Piave, on the Piave River between Venice and Trieste, and put up at the 'Albergo Leone Bianca', or 'White Lion Inn', as it would have been called in England.

I also remember eating a delicious lunch of hot bread, made from yellow polenta, with gorgonzola and washed down by a straw-covered bottle of Chianti, alongside the road somewhere near Padua that day. In contrast, outside Italy there was not much evidence of any 'wine of the country' being readily available for travellers and perhaps partly because of this, we drank very little alcohol of any kind during our journey.

The morning was warm and sunny when we came to the port city of Trieste, at the head of the Adriatic which had been annexed by Italy from the Austrians after the First World War. The town seemed to be full of holiday makers as we sat and ate our lunch in the sun by the harbour. Afterwards we procured some traveller's cheques in Yugoslavian *dinars* and climbed away from the sea, through the rough limestone country of the Carso, 'rather desolate and covered with low scrub', as my diary described it.

We passed through Postumia, where there was a large garrison watching over the road into Italy from the north-east and then the good Italian road stopped dead at Caccia on the Yugoslav frontier late in the afternoon. Straightaway we found ourselves on the kind

In Ljubljana, Yugoslavia.

The first Yugoslav village we encountered.

GB

Our first Balkan camp off the road to Zagreb.

of pot-holey gravel that we were used to in Australia and began to realise that at last we were no longer tourists, but travellers.

The first Yugoslav town of consequence that we came to was Ljubljana, situated not far south of the Austrian border and, as I recall, a pleasant city, dominated by a fortress built on a huge rock in its centre; though perhaps it was the spelling of the name that impressed us as much as anything; being then unaccustomed to the Slavonic 'j's. A few miles out along the road to Zagreb, we found our ideal camping spot, in a meadow just outside a village which had an 'onion' spire on the church, and there we felt that at last we had reached the Balkans.

A village in northern Yugoslavia.

Next day found us travelling through farming country with villages of small houses, with white-washed walls and roofs of half-round terracotta tiles, straggling along a gravel road — 'well laid out, but rough' — which wound down the valley of the Sava River. We stopped for a while at a village fair and market, where for us the main interest lay in the picturesque costumes of the crowd, which we photographed with mixed success.

By mid-afternoon we were in Zagreb, where we procured some bread, cheese, and a fresh supply of fuel, having made a note in the logbook that at that time we had finished our tanks of Swiss petrol, which was cheaper, and also better than the Italian variety. Zagreb we noted as being a large and attractive town with wide streets and good buildings, though we did not know then that it was also a university city, nor that, under its former name of 'Agram', it had been important as the capital of the Province of Croatia and Slavonia in the old Austro-Hungarian Empire before 1918.

We camped some miles east of Zagreb, near a large village named Klostar and, as we lay in bed reading by the light of a small bulb connected to the car battery, two soldiers, with rifles at the ready, entered the tent. Having no common language, communication was difficult, but when we produced our passports, they seemed to be satisfied and left us in peace; but well aware that we were now in an atmosphere much less free and easy than we had been used to at home in Australia.

A boy and his load in a Balkan village.

Early the next day we turned north from the Sava into hilly country again, through the village of Pakrac and east through the hills to the town of Pozega, where we indulged ourselves by having a lunch of tasty goulash at an open air cafe in the main square. Late that afternoon we reached the Drava River (which runs south-east and forms part of the boundary between Yugoslavia and Hungary) at Osijek, not far from the Drava's junction with the Danube. Here we had the first of our many punctures and decided to change over to our heavy tyres on the back wheels.

Now we were in the open country of the Danubian plain with large fields of stubble or ripening grain that reminded us of the best of Australian agricultural land. All the next day we travelled across this fertile plain, seeing cattle and sheep, as well as pigs, on the stubble fields, and taking some photographs at a pig market (where the animals were of a peculiar long-haired breed) and of the farmers in their light four-wheeled waggons, generally drawn by a pair of smart horses and capable of moving at a brisk pace, in spite of running on steel-tyred wooden wheels and having no springing between the axles and the wooden seats.

Gradually, we were leaving the country of the Croat peoples, where the Latin alphabet was used, and entering the old kingdom of Serbia. Here the sign posts were written in the Russian (Cyrillic) script and so were quite mysterious to us, a problem that

Country folk on their way to market with baskets to sell, Danubian Plain.

we would encounter often, until we reached India and came again under the influence of the English language.

Late in the afternoon of the following day we arrived at Belgrade; first built in very ancient times as a fortress on the high ground at the junction of the Sava and Danube rivers. Because of its importance as the key to the long line of communication along the Danube between Vienna and Constantinople (or between West and East) it had been the scene of prolonged sieges and savage battles between European Christian armies and the invading Moslem Turks, from the tenth century right through to the nineteenth.

There was an International Exhibition in progress when we were there and we had trouble in finding a place to stay. However, two cordial Yugo-Slavs took us to some lodgings and we ate our evening meal at a pavement cafe and watched a torch light procession, which my diary says was 'to do with a Balkan Olympiad'. The next morning we visited the International Exhibition, which mostly consisted of industrial exhibits that did not interest us much, and started on the road again in the afternoon, after what the diary described as 'trouble with the landlady', the nature of which I can't now recall.

One of the few recollections that I have of Belgrade is of a big road junction, where several streets met. The traffic was controlled by a single policeman standing on a small rostrum and, as each vehicle approached the intersection, the driver indicated to this man which way he wanted to go (it was before the days of blinkers) by sounding his horn a certain number of times — one for straight ahead, two to turn left, three to go right and so on. The din was terrific, but the cop seemed to be somehow able to sort out the drivers' intentions and to keep the traffic (which was not heavy) moving in spite of it.

We made camp thirty miles out from the city, after stopping briefly at a village fair to take photographs of the people in their best embroidered costumes, and next morning we turned south up the Morava River valley. The country became hilly again and there is mention in the diary of grapes growing on the ridges. Soon we had our second puncture of the trip and, while we were mending it, we were approached by a man who lived alongside the road and who, after a rather one-sided conversation, insisted that I should take a drink of some very strong and rather vile-tasting greenish liquid, probably a local variety of grappa, which he poured from a black bottle into my enamel mug. I found it quite an effort to swallow this mysterious offering, and after drinking it, I told Ted that I thought he had better drive. In fact I felt no ill effects and never doubted that our visitor was being hospitable.

That afternoon, still in the Morava valley, we passed through the old town of Nis (pronounced 'Nish') which is described as having had 'a conspicuous place in the Turkish wars from 1375 down to 1878', though I noted it at the time only as being a 'smallish place with a few good new buildings'. Here we photographed a group of women sitting on the edge of the pavement with baskets of fruit or vegetables in front of them, who, while they waited for buyers and talked amongst themselves, continued to spin woollen thread onto wooden spindles held in their right hands, teasing it out with the fingers of their left hands from a bundle of wool attached to a short stick strapped to their left wrists — the 'distaff side'.

We camped the night 'in a steep and desolate sort of valley by a stream' and late next morning, at the village of Bela Palanka, we each bought a pair of the peculiar peasant

Imbibing some local grappa with friends, thirty miles from Belgrade.

A street market for fruit and vegetables in the Serbian town of Nis, Morava Valley.

Peasants at a village fair in southern Yugoslavia, wearing curious long-toed soft leather shoes.

Workman at the Dragoman Pass, Bulgaria.

shoes, made from a single piece of leather, plaited round the insteps and drawn up at the toes into a raised point, that we had seen country people wearing through much of Yugoslavia. I kept mine for a good many years and wore them indoors as a novelty, but having no proper soles they were not very serviceable.

We crossed the Bulgarian frontier at Caribrod and then went through the rugged Dragoman Pass on a 'very rough and rocky road', which improved as the country opened out into farmland again when we approached Sofia, the capital, situated on another tributary of the Danube, in the late afternoon.

Sofia was a clean and well laid out small city, with wide streets and a spacious central square. We found a suitable hotel and in the late afternoon watched a procession of peasants, in town for a festival of some kind and wearing their party costumes, the women with embroidered skirts and short sleeveless jackets and the men in white shirts, embroidered waistcoats and tight trousers.

Next day we went to see the Dom (cathedral), which was Greek Orthodox and crowded for the festival and also the ornate little Russian Church, both very different in style and decoration from the familiar Gothic of the churches of Western Europe. So different in fact that, on a wall inside the Dom, there was painted a big mural that included the figure of God the Father, depicted as an old man with a white beard — rather like Santa Claus — an image that never seems to appear in Western churches.

At Sofia we were just 2000 miles and thirteen days actual travelling time out of London, which we reckoned would be about a quarter of the way to Calcutta; though in fact we had only a hazy idea of what the final distance would be.

Still, it was with some sense of achievement that we stocked up with Bulgarian money and other essentials in Sofia and took the road towards Plovdiv. This led us on a detour southward into rough hills by way of Samakov, over 'a very bad track', which changed for the better when we came out of the hills into the wide valley of the Maritza River.

We were now out of the Danube Basin for the first time since we had entered Yugoslavia and on the edge of a fertile area which stretched eastward to the Black Sea, though the Maritza itself turns south into Turkey, to enter the Aegean as part of the border with Greece.

Plovdiv, under its old name of Philippopolis, had been a provincial capital in the Macedonian empires of Philip and Alexander, some centuries before the Christian era. In my old 1895 edition of *Chambers's Encyclopaedia*, (which I have relied on a great deal for this kind of information) the city is described as having been 'ruined by the Goths, captured by the Turks (1363) destroyed by an earthquake (1818) burned (1846) and occupied by the Russians (1878)', but now, after so much destruction, it seemed to be an unremarkable town, where 'we put up at a small and rather dirty pub'. I remember this pub especially because there we had to use a 'long drop' that consisted of a rail set across the top of a shaft that led from the first floor, straight down to the ground level — or even, as we hoped, well into the soil below it.

After leaving Plovdiv we were travelling on the parched flat plain of western Thrace, and in the logbook we noted that the people were becoming 'increasingly Turkish in appearance'; a description that applied more to their features and complexions than to their costumes, which were almost universally drab.

We crossed the Turkish frontier at Sevilengrad about three in the afternoon and were

The Dom, Sofia.

Our first sight of minarets outside Erdine, Turkey.

delighted by our first sight of minarets, rising amongst the telephone wires, as we approached Edirne.

Under its old name of Adrianople, after its founder, the Roman emperor Hadrian, who died in 138 AD, Edirne had been a city of importance in older times, both to the Romans and later to the Ottoman Turks, and it was still a considerable place, with several mosques and other large buildings, but with an overall air of dinginess about it.

It was getting late when we arrived there and we could not get to a bank to change any money into Turkish lira. On top of that, the engine was running badly, apparently because of a problem in the ignition, and the radiator was leaking as well, so we went on and camped on open downs outside the city.

In the morning we worked successfully to cure both these troubles, but decided to go back to Edirne for petrol, as well as money, and there, as I noted in my diary later, 'we heard the news that Mr Chamberlain had flown to Munich to see Herr Hitler about the Sudeten question, which is evidently very grave'; news that did nothing to allay our anxieties about the possible onset of another World War, which it was generally feared that Germany would be likely to win, thus achieving the domination of Europe, the British Empire, and perhaps in the end, as Hitler himself certainly believed, the world.

There was general concern in England then that the outbreak of war might be followed quickly by heavy air raids, the effects of which on the civilian population had been drastically demonstrated by the raids on Barcelona and on smaller towns like Guernica, which had been carried out by German and Italian bombers in the Spanish Civil War only the year before. All of which was specially worrying to me, having left a sister just married and living in London and my fiancée at least temporarily there as well.

It began to rain in the afternoon as we drove eastward on a tarred road, so we had a wet camp on the black soil plain alongside it. We broke camp in the dark and, after some early problems with the sticky mud, which stuck to the wheels in great lumps, we drew out onto the road again, just as dawn began to break.

We stopped after sunrise for breakfast and a shave, on top of a low ridge in distant sight of the fabled city of Constantinople, now called Istanbul, capital of two empires during the last fifteen hundred years: firstly the Roman Empire of the East and then the Ottoman Turkish Empire and which for so long had been our goal as we travelled across Europe.

Our first stop when we reached the city was at the post office, but to our (especially my) disappointment there were no letters from home or loved ones. Then we went to a bank to draw a supply of lira for the long road ahead against our 'letters of credit', and finally to the British Consulate to find out more about the rules for travel in Turkey and to hear the latest reports about the crisis in Europe, concerning which in fact, there seemed to be little that was new during the last two days.

For our accommodation we took a room in the ornate, but rather shabby, 'Turing Palaz Oteli' in Pera, which was the business centre of the city, on the northern shore of the long narrow inlet, running west out of the Bosphorus, called the Golden Horn and spanned by the Galata Bridge.

On the southern side of the Horn was Stamboul, once the fortified part of the ancient city of Byzantium, which had stood on a broad point of land on the European side of the entrance to the Straits of the Bosphorus, guarding the passage to the Black Sea from the Aegean and hence the Mediterranean.

Constantinople had taken its name from its founder, the Roman Emperor Constantine the Great, who, in 330 AD, moved the capital of his empire from Rome to a site beside Byzantium, the city which had itself been founded some hundreds of years before as a Greek colony.

Since the time of its origin, Constantinople is said to have undergone no fewer than twenty-six sieges and been captured eight times, and of these captures, that by the Latins of the Fourth Crusade in 1204 is described as being 'by far the most disastrous and barbarous' of them all.

Its final conquest by the Ottoman Turks, perhaps made easier by the great damage to its defences wrought by the 'crusaders', took place in the year 1453, and they have ruled there ever since.

The rain fell heavily when we arrived in Istanbul, but cleared in the afternoon, so we hastened out to see some of the sights of the city.

First of these for us were the three great mosques, Hagia (Saint) Sophia, the Mosque of Sulieman and the Mosque of Sultan Ahmet (the 'Blue' Mosque) which stand almost beside one another, along the ridge above the western side of the city, looking over it across the Bosphorus to the 'suburb' of Scutari (or 'Uskudar' as the Turks call it) on the Asian side, where Florence Nightingale laboured in her hospital during the Crimean War in the 1850s.

Next morning we went back across the Galata Bridge to Stamboul for another look at the mosques, especially the Hagia Sophia, built in the sixth century as a Christian church by the Roman emperor Justinian and dedicated by him, not to a particular saint, but to the concept of 'Holy Wisdom'.

Unlike the Blue Mosque, whose walls are beautifully decorated with intricate patterns in blue tiles, the interior of San Sophia is relatively plain, but it stands under a huge dome, which is quite breath-taking in its effect, and which rivals in size the domes of St Paul's in London or St Peter's in Rome, though very much older than either of them.

The structure of the dome is supported on four enormous pillars of stone blocks, bound together with lead, and standing in a square 31 metres (101 feet) along the sides, which is also roughly the diameter of the dome's base, while the height from the floor to its crown is no less than 56 metres, or 182 feet — about the same as a fifteen-story building.

After nearly a thousand years as a Christian church and five centuries as a Mohammedan mosque, Hagia Sophia is now, since the 1930s and the rule of Kemal Ataturk, of whom more later, a national monument and museum.

Briefly we also saw the remains of the old Roman wall that had been part of the original fortifications of Stamboul, and then walked back through a corner of the huge covered bazaar, which has an area of many acres and contains nearly three thousand shops or stalls. Knowing something of this, we did not venture far into its maze of streets and alleys, of which there are several miles, because we had to return to the hotel in time to repack the car for the next leg of the trip.

This would be our entry into Asia; a new and exciting continent, where we felt sure that we would find experiences quite different from those of the European world.

The Golden Horn, Istanbul, seen from the river busy with a variety of craft.

Loading our car for the voyage down the Bosphorus to Mudanya.

Steaming down the Bosphorus after leaving Istanbul.

So it was with great anticipation that we watched the Morris being hoisted up from the wharf and swung onto the deck of the small modern ship, which ran the ferry service southward across the Sea of Marmara to the further shore of Turkey — Asia Minor at last!

In the late afternoon we steamed down the Bosphorus, the domes and minarets of the three big mosques silhouetted against the western sun, with the squalor of the city below them hidden in the light smoky haze that hung over the whole scene.

It was a memorable last glimpse of Europe.

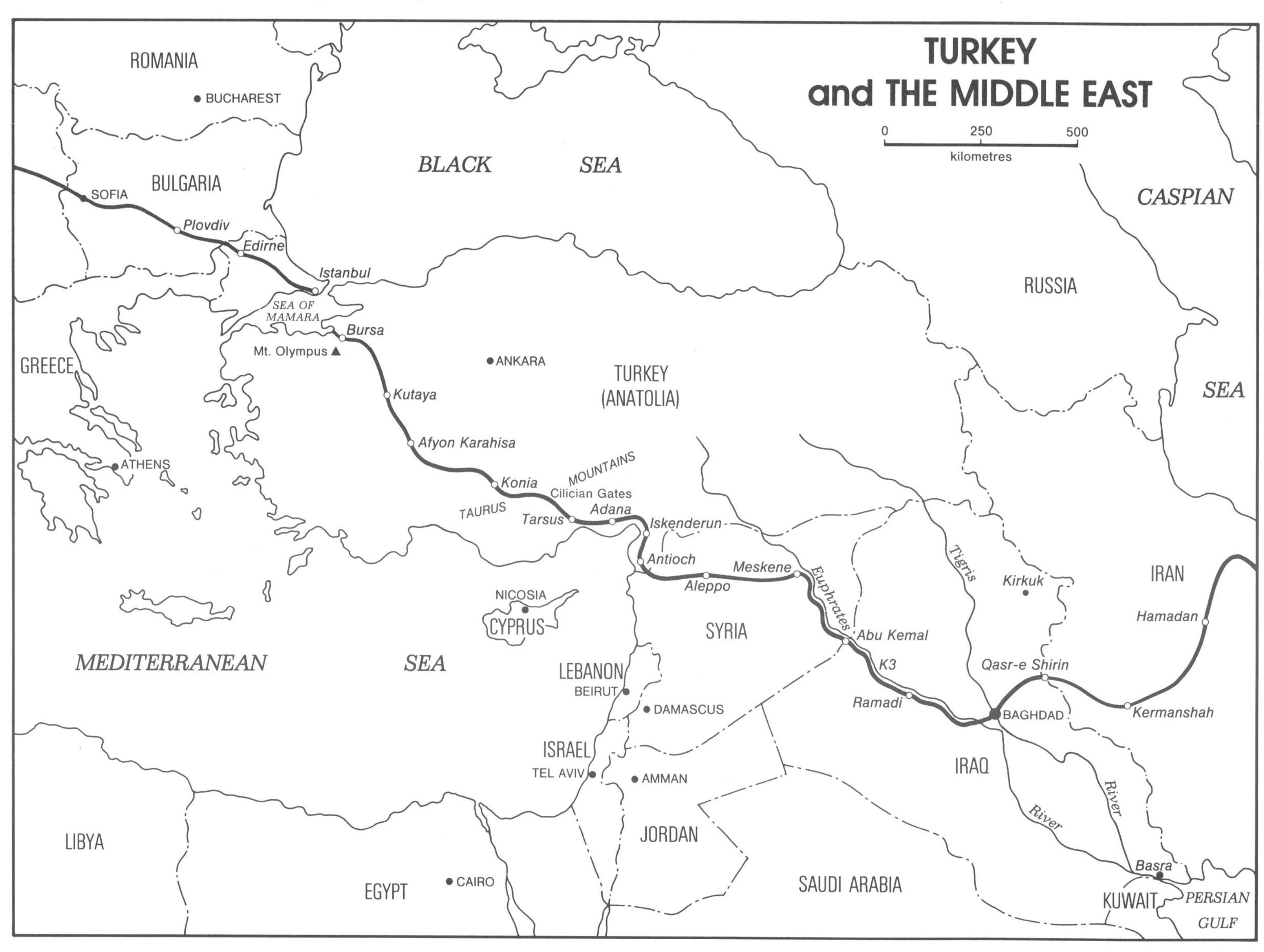
TURKEY
and THE MIDDLE EAST
0
250
500
kilometres
ROMANIA
BUCHAREST
BULGARIA
SOFIA
Plovdiv
Edirne
Istanbul
BLACK SEA
CASPIAN SEA
RUSSIA
SEA OF MAMARA
Bursa
Mt. Olympus
ANKARA
TURKEY (ANATOLIA)
GREECE
ATHENS
Kutaya
Afyon Karahisa
Konia
MOUNTAINS
TAURUS
Cilician Gates
Tarsus
Adana
Iskenderun
Antioch
Aleppo
Meskene
Euphrates
Tigris
Kirkuk
IRAN
Hamadan
NICOSIA
CYPRUS
SYRIA
Abu Kemal
K3
Ramadi
Qasr-e Shirin
BAGHDAD
Kermanshah
MEDITERRANEAN SEA
LEBANON
BEIRUT
DAMASCUS
ISRAEL
TEL AVIV
AMMAN
IRAQ
River
River
JORDAN
LIBYA
EGYPT
CAIRO
SAUDI ARABIA
Basra
KUWAIT
PERSIAN GULF

2

TURKEY AND THE MIDDLE EAST

The ship berthed at the small port of Mudanya, on the north-western coast of Asia Minor, in the early evening, after a smooth three-hour passage from Istanbul across the Sea of Marmara. After the car was unloaded on to the wharf we drove a few miles inland and made camp on a ridge overlooking the resort town of Bursa, which lay in a pleasant valley at the foot of a high mountain range.

The weather was overcast in the morning when we drove into Bursa for supplies and it did not clear as we climbed out of the valley on a very bad road, so that we could not see much of the mountain range nor of its main feature, the Ulu Dagh, partly hidden in the cloud above our heads, but according to our map, nearly 8000 feet (2495 metres) high and named Mount Olympus. This was, as we discovered later, one of several mountains which the ancient Greeks referred to by that name, the best known one, famous as the dwelling-place of the gods, being in Thessaly in northern Greece.

Passing a young shepherd on the Anatolian plain.

The foothills of the Ulu Dagh were steep and rough, with a cover of low scrub, and the road became worse as we followed it south-east over a series of ridges to the little town of Inegol. We ate our lunch just beyond the town and then climbed over another range to Karakoy and up a narrow valley between barren hills, passing a caravan of donkeys and hairy two-humped Bactrian camels camped beside the track. After passing Bozoyuk we ran into a stretch of heavy mud, in which we very nearly stuck, and then turned south off the 'main' road, which continued eastward through Eskisehir towards the capital Ankara, still shown on our map under its old name of Angora. The road did not improve as we climbed further, being alternately muddy, or rough and stony, and we were glad finally to make camp for the night on a cold and windy basalt ridge.

We were now on the Anatolian Plateau, which has a general height of between four and six thousand feet (1400 to 2000 metres) above sea level, and for the next few days we saw mainly treeless steppes covered with rough grass, varied only by small patches of low scrub and sometimes intersected by areas of salt marsh. There was not much cultivation and the land seemed poor and thinly populated when compared with the wide and fertile valleys of the Balkans, which we had travelled through during the previous week.

Occasionally we saw small flocks of fat-tailed Karakul sheep of various colours, sometimes running with goats, which were usually black. Often the shepherd would include a single donkey with his flock, apparently to act as its leader. Donkeys were also the usual

The road out of Bozoyuk was muddy and soft.

pack or riding animals used by the peasant farmers who scratched a meagre living off the land and dwelt in the few small local villages.

This was the real heartland of Turkey, peopled by the tough Anatolian peasants who had made up the bulk of the army that had fought so stubbornly during the Gallipoli campaign and in Palestine against the Allies, including the Anzacs, during the First World War and in the process earned the grudging, but sincere, respect of the troops who had opposed them.

In 1938, the Turkish people were still wrestling with the drastic, though undoubtedly beneficial, changes that had been forced on them during the preceding fifteen years by the then president-for-life of the Turkish Republic and its virtual dictator, Kemal Ataturk. It was he who, as Mustafa Kemal Pasha, had commanded an infantry division on Gallipoli and who, because of his swift response to the Allied landings of 25 April 1915 and his leadership and tactical skill in the desperate battles that followed, was credited with holding back the enemy's attacks until they lost their impetus and finally failed to establish a secure position astride the peninsula. In the end, after nearly ten months of bloody warfare, and at a total cost of half a million casualties (in about equal numbers on either side and of whom at least a hundred thousand died) the Allies were forced to abandon their hard-won footholds on Turkish soil. Their final victory in the war against the Ottoman Empire took place three years later, on other fronts, and again at tremendous cost.

As a result of their earlier defeats in the Balkan Wars of 1911—12, the Turks had already lost control of much of their former territory in Europe, which then included most of what is now Bulgaria and northern Greece. Now, having backed the German side in the First World War, the Turks were again the losers and in 1920, under the Treaty of Sevres, the Allies imposed even more drastic peace terms on Turkey, which deprived it of control over all its possessions in the Middle East. Among these had been Syria, Palestine, Iraq and Arabia. Worse still, they also handed to Greece territory on the western end of Asia Minor, opposite the Dodecanese Islands and including the port and province of Smyrna, now called Izmir.

These losses had a drastically destabilising effect on the government of the Sultan in Constantinople, and when the Greeks tried to follow their successes at the conference table with an incursion into the centre of Anatolia through Smyrna in 1921, it was left to Kemal Pasha to rally the Turkish army sufficiently to defeat them, first on the Sakarya River in front of Angora and finally further south and west of there, near Konya.

His victories caused a revision of the Allied opinion of Turkey's ability to fight back from apparent defeat, so that, by the ensuing Treaty of Lausanne, signed in 1923, she regained control of the whole of Asia Minor, together with eastern Thrace between Edirne and Constantinople on the European side of the Bosphorus. The country thus substantially assumed its present form, with Kemal at its head.

He had set up the base for his resistance to the Greeks at Angora, then a small remote city in the middle of Anatolia, and because of his distrust of the 'Europeanising' influence of Constantinople (which he re-named Istanbul) and also for strategic reasons, decided that Angora (now Ankara) should be the capital of the new Republic of Turkey.

This republic he was determined to develop as a modern secular state, quite unlike

Lunch outside Kutahya, on a cold, windswept plain.

the almost feudal rule of the old 'Sublime Porte', which had been built on the concept of the Sultan as the Caliph of Islam, combining in his person both temporal and religious powers.

A Turkish woman wearing the previously common dress of trousers.

A village near Konya.

Kemal proceeded to create a whole new system of government based on Western lines, under which women were to have (officially at least) equal status with men and should go unveiled in public. Everyone was to wear 'modern' clothes including, for the men, European-style hats or caps instead of the traditional red fez. Education was to be universal and non-religious and a new alphabet based on the Latin model, with some modifications said to have been devised by Ataturk himself, would take the place of the old Arabic script which, he was convinced, had prevented the Turks from joining the mainstream of Western culture.

All this made a formidable program of change, and for us one obvious effect was that the whole population seemed to be dressed in drab and undistinguished clothes that tended to look as though they were someone else's castoffs. Only once, and that was out in the country, did we catch a glimpse of (and hastily photographed) a woman wearing the traditional baggy Turkish trousers. The men mostly wore dark caps with small shiny peaks, and the bright red fez was nowhere to be seen.

Nevertheless, Ataturk (the name meant Father of the Turks) had carried out his many changes relentlessly, though not brutally, so that by 1938, after fifteen years of law reform and firm government, he had achieved the status of being both the national hero and the father-figure of his nation.

Ted and I had a special interest in Turkey because two of our mutual uncles, Bertram and Maurice Delpratt, had been in the Gallipoli campaign, and Maurice had been taken prisoner there after he had stumbled into a trench full of Turks while out on reconnaissance between the lines.

His own account of this incident, in a letter to his family, included the rueful reflection that the only words of Turkish that he had been taught called on the enemy to surrender to *him*.

He spent three and a half years as a prisoner of war, mostly at work on building the railway south from Konya (the Roman 'Iconium') towards the Mediterranean, including a tunnel through the Taurus Mountains. By Maurice's account in his letters home, his treatment by the Turks was relatively humane, given the circumstances of a harsh climate and the fact that his captors were themselves accustomed to few, if any, comforts.

It took us almost a week to cross Asia Minor, and most of the time we had no accurate way of telling what was happening in Europe; whether Hitler was about to begin the war that most people by now believed he was determined to embark upon, while Britain and France sought to thwart his plans for the further expansion of the Third Reich.

Our isolation from the local inhabitants was almost complete because of language difficulties. Ted spoke some German and I had my school French, which enabled me to read or write that language in simple form, but was of little use in spoken conversation. English hardly seemed to exist as a means of communication in Anatolia at that time and, although the Turkish newspaper that we saw in Konya was (thanks to Ataturk) at least printed in Latin script, the meaning of the text was almost incomprehensible to us.

A village cemetery near Kutaya.

The town of Afyon Karahisa.

However, as there were some smiling photographs of Chamberlain and Hitler with mysterious captions under them, we reckoned that the war had not yet begun.

We had no radio in the car with which to listen to the BBC World Service, as one might do now, but on the whole we did not mind too much, well knowing that we had no choice but to keep going whatever happened, at least until we reached the Mediterranean coast.

The next town we saw, after our cold camp on the stony ridge on that second night in Anatolia, was Kutahya, where we bought food and petrol and later stopped for lunch near an old Moslem cemetery, outside a small village set in bare, open hills. By mid-afternoon we were at the town of Afyon Karahisa, a name which translates as 'Opium Black Castle'. We knew that Uncle Maurice had been held here and had had a bad time, so we procured a postcard and sent it to him, as a reminder of former days.

Evidently the word *hisa* referred to a small citadel built in ancient times, perhaps by the Seljuk Turks, on a huge black rock beside the town and hardly visible from below. The opium poppies, if they were still being grown, had all been harvested by then (late September) so that the photographs Ted took show only a little town of flat-roofed mud-brick houses, huddled against a low range of rocky hills.

It was a forbidding-looking place and we could well understand that, when Maurice wrote later in his captivity of 'the bad old days at Afyon', he was perhaps referring to the climate and the prevalence of malaria, from which many prisoners died, as much as to his treatment by the Turks.

The road improved after we left Afyon and ran south-east, with a range of hills on our right and a wide swampy plain on our left. The mosquitoes were bad when we made camp in another stony field alongside the road, but we were well pleased with our day's run of 150 miles.

Our luck changed next morning after we passed through Aksehir. On a section of road marked on our map with the expressive word *piste*, we drove into heavy mud that collected under the mudguards and stopped us from moving until we dug the car out. We suffered another puncture near Ilgin, but after that the road improved again, and under a fine evening sky we camped on open downs not far from Konya.

Here we received our first Turkish visitor, a good-looking lad of about sixteen, accompanied by a big creamy-coloured dog with black points and wearing a collar bristling with iron spikes at least an inch long. These, we understood, were designed to protect its throat from being torn by wolves while it guarded its master's flock of sheep. We had an agreeable conversation, mostly in sign language, from which we gathered that the boy's name was Mustafa Turqut and that his dog was called Sari. It seems very likely that Sari was one of the Anatolian breed called *Karabash*, meaning 'black-faced', which are renowned as guard dogs for sheep (or other animals or things to which they become 'bonded') even when they are left quite alone to watch over their charges.

Early the next morning Mustafa was back again to be photographed, and he laboriously wrote his name and address on an envelope so that we could send him a copy of his picture from Australia. Unfortunately, because at the time it seemed unlikely that the

A typical shepherd near Konya, Anatolia.

Salt steppes near Konya.

The 'road' leading into an Anatolian village.

Australian post office would understand such a roughly pencilled inscription, the envelope was filed away with other memorabilia of the trip until recently, when with the help of a Turkish friend, it was rewritten and sent with a covering letter to the address given on the envelope. Thus far, alas, there has been no reply.

Mustafa Turqut with his dog, Sari.

Konya proved to be the biggest town we had seen since leaving Istanbul, with a military garrison that was about to have some artillery practice across the road as we came along. As Iconium it had been a provincial capital under the Roman Empire, important as a junction of trade routes through Asia Minor. St Paul visited it several times early in the Christian era and founded a Christian church there, while in the eleventh century it was the capital of the empire of the Seljuk Turks, forerunners of the Ottomans.

Much earlier, the climate of the Konya plains had been very different from its present dry and cold state, supporting forests and agriculture and a quite unexpectedly large population.

None of this was apparent to us as we did the usual shopping for *doner*, the unleavened Turkish bread, and some rice, eggs and melons, and bought the first newspaper we had seen since we left Istanbul. A man at a garage, who spoke a little English, gave us some vaguely reassuring news about the international situation.

We made good progress on fair roads over flat country until after we had passed through the town of Eregli, approaching the foothills of the Taurus Mountains, the Turkish name for which is the *Bulgar Dagh*. Here we hit a big pothole, hidden in the 'bull dust', which opened up a leak at the bottom of the radiator, so we decided to stop for the night and wait until the next day to repair the damage. This we eventually did, under the full sun, but soon we struck an even worse pothole, which had the effect of not only re-opening the leak, but also of displacing both front spring shackles and bending the main leaves of the springs themselves — the shock absorbers being none too effective on the Morris cars of that period — and we had to begin work all over again.

While we laboured on this exasperating job, a middle-aged peasant, driving a small donkey cart loaded with melons, pulled up alongside the car. After silently watching us for a while, without attempting any conversation, he got down from the cart and unloaded two choice melons, which he left beside us in a mute gesture of sympathy. It was a touching act from one who seemed to appreciate the problems of being a traveller, and we did our best to convey how grateful we felt towards him.

At the same time we were reminded of the contrast between his attitude and one of Maurice's grimmer stories from the same area. How, while following down a gully in search of water for a party of fellow prisoners travelling on a train, he had come upon two corpses, their hands tied and with bullet wounds in the backs of their heads; Armenians, he presumed, who were then the oppressed minority in Turkey.

Finally we got things back into place again and chocked up the damaged springs with wooden blocks, which had a bad effect on the riding and steering qualities of the car. In spite of this we continued our rather uncertain way eastward, along a rough winding road in the foothills of the Taurus, with snow on the ranges to our right.

We were looking for a village called Ulu Kisla, which we found to be 'a small, dirty place in a valley at the foot of the Bulgar Dagh'. Here the road turned south up the

The Cilician Gates in the Taurus Mountains.

valley and we camped that night between it and the railway-line, probably near the tunnel that Uncle Maurice had helped to build. More snow was showing on the mountains ahead of us, not far from the little town of Posanti, where next morning we went through a passport check, though still many miles from the frontier.

Posanti stood near the top of the pass known as the Cilician Gates, the ancient route through the Taurus between Anatolia and the Mediterranean coast, used alike by merchant caravans and by Christian missionaries such as St Paul, or by the army of Alexander the Great, who had come this way in 333 BC, leading his Macedonians against the invading hordes of the Persian King Darius III.

Perhaps Alexander's passage was commemorated by the Greek inscription we saw cut into the rock wall of a narrow defile through which the road ran after crossing the pass, and which we supposed marked the actual Gates themselves. And perhaps this was the spot that so impressed the traveller who wrote in 1910, 'This is the veritable Gate of Cilicia. A double door would close it and defy an army.'

We would have stopped to examine the lettering more closely and photograph it, but for the fact that we were at that time hurrying in pursuit of two camels that we had accidentally started down the road away from their owner. To make up for this lack of road manners, we felt obliged to pick the man up, along with his small child, and with the father standing on the car's running board and the child in with us, to go as hard as we could until we managed to head the animals further along the narrow road.

The top of the pass itself (3770 feet—1160 metres) was relatively open, with wide views back down the valley to the north, and after we went through the Gates and began

The top of the Pass leading to the Cilician Gates, where a thin line of telegraph poles marches across the countryside.

to descend on the southern side by rough and winding cuttings, we could see ahead of us the coastal plain and beyond that a thrilling glimpse of the blue Mediterranean.

Late in the afternoon we reached Tarsus, birthplace of the apostle Paul and once the capital of the Roman province of Cilicia, built on the flat country at the foot of the mountains. 'Not much of a town' we noted in the logbook, but we were pleased to see that someone had planted Australian eucalypt trees along the streets. Tarsus stands on the bands of the Cydnus, one of the three rivers that run down to the Mediterranean from the Taurus Range across the Cilician Plain, and it was up the Cydnus that Cleopatra travelled in her 'purple sailed galley' to lay herself at the feet of Mark Anthony in 41 BC.

We, however, could not afford the time to dwell on that romantic scene, so we left Tarsus and camped a few miles out on the road that ran east towards the town of Adana, with a fine view of the Taurus Mountains to the north across the plain.

Not far beyond Adana, near Missis, we photographed the best-preserved of several ruined stone castles, strategically placed on hills overlooking and commanding the passage between the mountains and the sea. Looking at the remains of its massive stone walls and the typically Norman style of its architecture, we supposed that it might have been built by some disgruntled Crusader who had decided to set himself up as an unofficial guardian of the road and then no doubt to levy tribute from its users in return for his 'protection'.

An hour later we came to the village of Toprakkale and here we turned south through a gap in the hills on to the Plain of Issus, overlooked by another ruined castle (also called

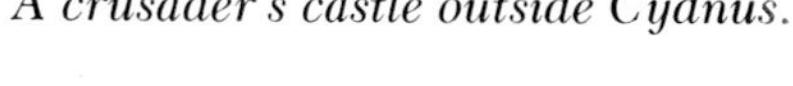

A crusader's castle outside Cydnus.

Ruins of the castle outside Toprakkale.

Toprakkale) and built in the tenth century by a Byzantine emperor. We scrambled up the slope to the castle to examine what was left of its huge walls and arches and to gaze out through them at the waters of the Gulf of Alexandretta (as it was then called) shining beyond the plain.

On this same plain, hemmed in between the mountains and the sea, was fought, in 333 BC, one of the great battles of ancient times, when the armies of Alexander finally met those of Darius on the banks of one of the small rivers that flow west from the Amanus Mountains into the gulf.

Estimates of the size of these armies are sure to be unreliable, but it seems likely that Alexander's Macedonians numbered at least 30,000, while the troops of Darius, which included contingents from the many nations of the Persian Empire, were much more numerous (one estimate even says 600,000, which must be wildly exaggerated.) Both sides included cavalry, but in the end the tactical skill and equipment of the Macedonian troops prevailed and Darius fled in his chariot, leaving behind not only much treasure, but also his family and his generals.

These Alexander is said to have treated 'magnanimously', as he advanced on his triumphant march through Syria, Egypt and (still pursuing Darius) finally into Persia itself, where he burnt Persepolis and led his army on through what is now Afghanistan. He went as far east as the Punjab in India, before returning with the remnants of his troops to Persia, and thence to his capital Babylon, in Mesopotamia, where he died in 323 BC, at the age of only thirty-two.

Ted and I knew only a little of all this when we took the road that led us along the shores of the gulf towards the then Turkish frontier at Payas, where we camped for the

Ted at the gate of Toprakkale Castle.

Owen with a young Dutch adventurer at the Turkish-Syrian frontier.

night before crossing into Syria. Instead we took pleasure in seeing that here, in the softer climate of the Mediterranean coastal plain, now only about a mile wide, there were orchards of oranges and figs, while olive groves extended up the slopes of attractive hills.

It was a great contrast to the Anatolian steppes.

The weather was sunny and warm when we passed through the Turkish customs, and there we encountered our first fellow traveller — a young Dutchman, who was riding a light motorbike and who told us that he was on his way to Egypt. Then he hoped to go right through to the Dutch East Indies (now Indonesia), which seemed to be almost too ambitious a goal.

From Payas the road ran along the edge of the bay into the town of Alexandretta itself (now called by the Turks Iskenderun or 'Alexander's town') which was then a port for northern Syria, but which was returned to Turkey, along with Antioch (now Antakya) just before World War Two.

We ate lunch in the sun on a ridge overlooking the town and the sea and then turned inland across the steep range of the Amanas Mountains on the road to the old biblical city of Antioch, once the capital of the Greek, and later the Roman, rulers of Syria. Under the latter, during the first three centuries AD, the importance of the city increased to the point where it was said to have contained 500,000 inhabitants and to have rivalled even Rome in its splendour, being described as the 'Crown of the East' and the 'chief city of Asia.'

Syria was now a French Mandated Territory, having been handed over to France as its share of the spoils from the split up of the Ottoman Empire after the First World War. As a consequence we found that the roads were very much better there than they had been in Turkey, and we made the journey to Antioch in good time that afternoon. Like many other cities that we visited, Antioch, after centuries of siege and conquest, showed few signs of its former grandeur, nor of its importance as an early stronghold of the new faith of Christianity, and we passed through it with only brief recorded comment.

Of more immediate concern to us was the fact that, with a following wind, the engine overheated again as we climbed up out of the fertile valley of the Orontes River, which ran beside the city, and began to 'scream', as it had done in Italy. This decided us to stop and make camp for the night when we came to the top of the ridge, near an old Roman arch spanning the road not far from Sermada, on the way to Aleppo.

Next morning we drove over what appeared to be the remains of a Roman road, formed from big squared paving stones, and after an hour's travel we reached Aleppo, which we noted in the logbook as having 'many fine new buildings and signs of French influence.'

Indeed, even the British consul was himself a Frenchman, who took a very pessimistic view of the international situation and of Neville Chamberlain's negotiations with Hitler over Czecho-Slovakia and his return from Munich 'avec sa parapluie', a sour reference to the fact that the British Prime Minister was always depicted as carrying a rolled-up umbrella.

However, we were cheered by finding some mail for us poste restante at Aleppo, which reassured me at least, that I was not quite forgotten (it was just over three weeks since we had left Switzerland) and, after studying the local French newspaper to try to

A Roman arch on the way to Aleppo.

Transporting bales of cotton in Aleppo, along a beautifully paved street.

A water wheel on the Euphrates River.

Driving on the bed of the Euphrates near Meskene.

assess the chances of war breaking out in the near future, as well as the state of affairs in Palestine, we decided to take the road eastward towards the Euphrates.

This meant that we could avoid going south to Damascus and having then to make the long haul east across the Syrian desert by way of Rutbah Wells, which we would have had to do in convoy, with the chance of consequent delays. Instead, we would follow the river down to Baghdad from where, if things looked too bad on the European scene, we could divert to Basra, at the head of the Persian Gulf, and hopefully take a ship from there in the general direction of Australia.

Before leaving Aleppo we had the main leaves of both front springs replaced and then, fortified with fresh supplies from the greater variety of goods available in the city, we left in the early afternoon and drove east on a good gravel road over bare stony plains dotted with small villages of beehive-shaped houses. That night we camped on the flat banks of the Euphrates River near the small town of Meskene.

We got away in good time the following morning, watched by a small Arab audience, and all that day kept in contact with the river, either along smooth dusty tracks in the wide river bed itself, or out on the western bank over clay pans or low gravelly ridges, covered with a sparse growth of camel-thorn and similar bushes. There were a few small villages along the track and some flocks of fat-tailed sheep or goats tended by Arab boys whose fathers rode on very small donkeys, or sometimes on camels — the single-humped dromedaries of Arabia, universal throughout the hotter parts of the Middle East.

There was not much sign of irrigation, or any other form of agriculture, along this part of the Euphrates valley, except for occasional water-wheels, set up where the deep water ran close enough to the bank for them to be turned by the current and to empty their buckets into small aqueducts that carried the water back to gardens or orchards of date palms not far from the river.

Dromedaries ridden by Arab boys near the Euphrates.

Ted filling the tank in Meskene, surrounded by curious onlookers.

We passed the town of Deir ez Zor in the afternoon and camped near the village of Meyadin, about halfway to Baghdad, after a near-record run of 168 miles. There we spent some time on car maintenance before setting off next day. Later we stopped to look at some recent excavations on the site of a ruined city, named on the map as Salihiya, which evidently had walls of great height and enormous thickness. Unfortunately, there was no one on the job to tell us anything about the city's origins, or who was sponsoring the dig, so after looking round the site and taking some photographs, we set off down the river again. Later research by Ted revealed that this was the site of an old Roman fortified town, which then had the name of Dura Europus, and that in its ruins had been found 'important paintings of the Roman period' along with 'Greek parchments dating from well before Christ'.

Guard and attendants at the Syria-Iraqi border.

At Abu Kemal we crossed the frontier into Iraq; rather a lengthy business, only enlivened by the local Iraqi schoolmaster who was delighted to find someone on whom he could practise his English, while he helped us wash the dust from our throats with glasses of sweet black tea.

That evening we made camp in a dry *wadi*, about a hundred yards from the river, and here I decided to venture into the waters of the Euphrates for a much needed all-over wash, the first since Istanbul. It was not an enjoyable experience, partly because of the deep mud along the water's edge, but more so because the water itself, fed from the snows of the mountains of eastern Anatolia, was extremely cold. I came back to camp feeling virtuous but by no means clean, and Ted, after hearing my account of the situation, wisely decided to postpone his bathing until after we reached Baghdad.

Ted at Abu Kemal, Syria-Iraqui border.

Ruins of Dura Europa.

The next day we came to some large plantings of date palms, irrigated again by water-wheels, supported on stone arches that ran out into the stream. We were pleased to be able to add some delicious fresh dates to our usual rations of rice, unleavened bread and various canned goods.

We saw the first sign of what could be called Western influence since we had left Aleppo, when we entered the small group of huts that comprised the pumping station designated K3. This was one of several such stations on the pipeline that carried oil from the field at Kirkuk, westward some 600 miles across the desert to the port of Haifa on the Mediterranean coast. The pipeline belonged to the Iraqi Petroleum Company, owned, or at least operated, by the British. Travellers were not such a novelty at K3 as to cause the staff to lay out any red carpets for us, but they were civil enough and it was nice to hear English spoken as a native tongue again. More importantly, the wireless operator was able to give us some authoritative news about the crisis in Europe, which was that Chamberlain and Hitler had signed the now notorious Munich Agreement; so I noted that 'the war scare seems off for the present', even though the wireless operator said we'd backed down to Hitler.

The next day we passed by the old walled city of Hit.

Its name was probably a relic of the ancient Hittites, a people often mentioned in the Old Testament, because of their association with the Children of Israel from the time of Abraham onwards. Their origins are uncertain, but they established a kingdom in Anatolia and northern Syria in Neolithic times, more than two thousand years before the time of Christ. The remains of two of their cities, Hartusa, east of Ankara, and Catal

Huyuk, under a huge flat mound on the plain near Konya, are still being excavated, yielding evidence of a numerous population and a high level of culture previously unknown to archaeologists, thus emphasising the great changes in climate and vegetation that must have taken place in that part of the world since then.

The Hittites fought intermittent wars with the Egyptians, their southern neighbours, and they won a great battle against them at Qadesh, near Homs in Syria, in about 1600 BC. One reason for their victory is said to have been that the Hittite chariots were bigger and heavier than those of their opponents and carried three men, while the Egyptians had only one man to defend the driver, as well as to attack the enemy. Besides this, the fact that both sides subsequently made a treaty, written on clay tablets, is regarded as something of a milestone in the history of international relations.

Junction of the roads to Baghdad from Damascus and Aleppo.

Not far south of Hit, we came to the junction of our road with the one coming east across the desert from Damascus by way of Rutbah Wells. Here Ted photographed the car alongside the signpost where the roads met, which was about 4000 'travelled' miles from London.

The road turned to bitumen after we passed through the modern-looking town of Ramadi and ran along the shore of Lake Habbaniyah, where the Royal Air Force maintained a base, at that time being used by the new Empire flying-boats on the service to Australia.

Not far from the aerodrome we crossed the Euphrates at El Fallouja and after travelling due east for another hour, mostly over a corrugated gravel road, we came to Baghdad, the capital of Iraq, crossing the Tigris River over a pontoon bridge inside the city limits — just under 600 miles out of Aleppo.

As usual we made for the post office, but when we got there it was shut, so we retraced our tracks along the Ramadi road and made camp outside the city. We came back to town the next morning and booked into the Hotel Astoria, a large, but rather run-down three-storey building in Al-Raschid Street. This was Baghdad's main thoroughfare, named after the Caliph Haroun Al-Raschid, ruler of the city in the ninth century, whose name is associated with the famous *Tales of a Thousand and One Nights*, which were supposedly set in Baghdad.

It was a long and rather narrow street, running roughly parallel with the river and crowded with buses and trucks that filled the air with strange smelling fumes, unlike any we had encountered before. The standard of architecture was disappointingly low and the atmosphere far from romantic, which we felt should have been a feature of the city of the Arabian Nights.

We did see in the Museum a wonderful collection of artefacts from the then quite recently excavated sites of Babylon and Ur of the Chaldees, both situated in Mesopotamia, the 'cradle of civilisation', between the Tigris and Euphrates rivers, not far south from Baghdad. It was quite strange to feel that we were looking at the handiwork of men who had lived perhaps 5000 years before, close to where we were standing.

The day was very hot, so we repaired to the hotel to enjoy the luxury of an afternoon siesta and to wait for the worst of the heat to go out of the sun before taking in the sights of Baghdad: a stroll down Al Raschid Street, perhaps a mile, to the Maude Bridge over the Tigris and admiring the sunset there. Looking back now, it seems a pity that we did not go in search of more exciting experiences, but then we were too fully extended

In the old walled city of Hit, with camels for company.

already to be in any mood for venturing into the mysterious flesh-pots of the city, even if we had known where to start looking for them.

We did, however, enjoy a memorably huge seven-course dinner in near European style at the hotel that night, after which we wrote some letters before turning in. The sheets on the beds did not look very clean as we turned them back, but we were by then too tired to start an argument with the management about such niceties, and at least there actually were sheets, which was in itself a luxury.

After a busy day of car repairs (mainly extra leaves in the back springs), visits to the offices of the indispensible Thos Cook & Son, the post office and the Iranian Consulate (very reassuring as usual), it was early evening before we cleared the city on the road that ran north-east to the town of Khanaqin, near the Iranian border.

As we were settling down on to our stretchers after tea, in our camp in the desert about ten miles out of Baghdad, we were interrupted by two mounted Iraqi troopers who abruptly entered the tent and insisted that we must go with them. We could only understand the words 'bad Bedouin' and the descriptive action of a hand drawn across the throat in their impassioned speech. However, that was convincing enough for us, so we packed up and followed them to their headquarters: a small, two-storied mud-brick building, where we were comfortably lodged for the night in an upstairs room.

Next morning we were courteously sent on our way, after having been given the usual glasses (in the Arab fashion) of black tea — the *chai* of the Middle East — and having taken a group photograph outside the little fort. Because of the usual language problems, however, we were unable to discover who the 'bad Bedouin' might have been.

Ted takes early morning chai *at the Iraqi police post.*

Entries from the logbook for 2–3 October 1938.

At Baqubah, where there were irrigated plantations, we replenished our stock of dates by inducing a young Arab boy to climb a palm tree and cut down a bunch large enough to keep us supplied for several days.

It was just a hundred miles from Baghdad to Khanaqin, the last town before the Iranian border. The drive was easy, marred by only a single puncture, and the last thirty miles of the road were bitumen, something we would not see again until we were in India.

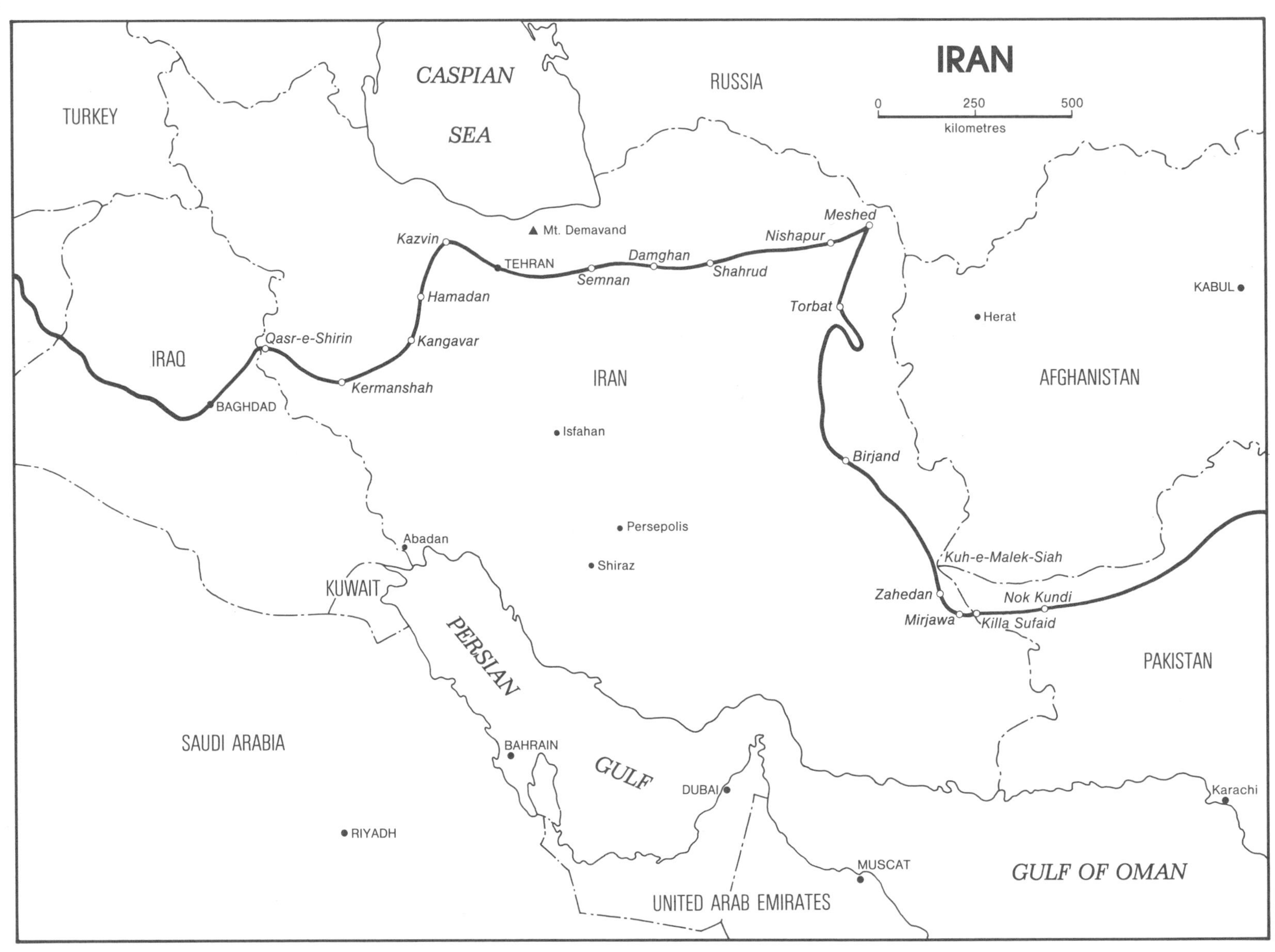
IRAN
0
250
500
kilometres
CASPIAN
SEA
RUSSIA
TURKEY
IRAQ
IRAN
AFGHANISTAN
PAKISTAN
KUWAIT
SAUDI ARABIA
PERSIAN
GULF
UNITED ARAB EMIRATES
GULF OF OMAN
Mt. Demavand
Kazvin
TEHRAN
Semnan
Damghan
Shahrud
Nishapur
Meshed
Torbat
Hamadan
Kangavar
Kermanshah
Qasr-e-Shirin
BAGHDAD
Isfahan
Persepolis
Shiraz
Abadan
Birjand
Kuh-e-Malek-Siah
Zahedan
Mirjawa
Killa Sufaid
Nok Kundi
Herat
KABUL
BAHRAIN
DUBAI
RIYADH
MUSCAT
Karachi

3

IRAN

There were delays at the Iranian frontier post near Qasr-e Shirin, a few miles beyond Khanaqin and, because it was getting late, we decided to make camp alongside the road. We were again moved on (less politely this time) by some Iranian soldiers, who took us to the police post outside the town.

These posts were to become a regular and unwelcome feature of our travels through Iran. Generally, each consisted of a small mud-brick hut set up alongside the road on the outskirts of all the larger towns and manned by two or three policemen dressed in pale blue uniforms with German-style spiked helmets. Their duty was to examine the papers and record the particulars of any travellers who passed by, whether entering the town or leaving it. Consequently we sometimes had to run the gauntlet of these investigations several times a day, which would not have been so bad in itself, apart from the waste of precious time for us, but was made more exasperating by the attitude of some of our interrogators.

Perhaps it was unfair to blame them too much, because obviously their standard of education was not high, even in Iranian terms, so it was no wonder that they had trouble in making sense out of words from a foreign language written in an unknown alphabet. They seemed to be able to write phonetic translations of our names if we read them out very carefully and slowly ('Why-et' and 'Wry-et') but when we tried to explain our occupations things became difficult. Ted, being described as an 'engineer', they could accept without much question, but I was listed as a 'grazier', and this mysterious word was apt to throw them into a state of suspicion and disbelief. The only way we could think of to explain its meaning was by waving our arms to describe large tracts of land covered with numerous sheep, which it was hard to do convincingly, especially as we were ourselves ignorant of the Iranian words for either of these things.

We negotiated the difficulties successfully, however, and being allowed to go on unhindered, we soon made camp by the roadside on the northern side of Qasr-e Shirin. We were still on relatively low land, and the night was comfortably warm, but ahead we could see the rugged hills that formed the base of the Iranian Plateau. Around us was an area of bare, eroded ridges, between which were wide valleys covered with long dry grass, sometimes divided by streams coming down from the hills, a few of which carried enough water to allow small-scale irrigation. In these valleys grazed flocks of fat-tailed Karakul sheep and some of the same breed of black goats that we had seen in Turkey.

The only trees visible on the landscape, apart from small patches of stunted scrub on the ridges, were some clumps of Lombardy poplars (surely the world's most widespread species) along the water courses.

These sparse timbers seemed to be the only likely sources of fuel for the people to use for cooking or for keeping warm, except for the bundles of camel-thorn that they laboriously collected and carried home on the backs of donkeys. Perhaps by then oil, in one form or another, may have been on sale in the villages for those able to afford it.

A donkey carrying camel thorn, a source of fuel.

We ourselves we were not once able to light a campfire on the whole of the trip because fuel was always so scarce and we had to rely entirely on our tiny petrol stove (which we called the 'hisser') to cook rice or boil the billy for tea or eggs. I don't remember ever having any fresh meat, though we did buy tins of bully beef at times, as well as cheese when available, which was very seldom once we left Europe. Fruit or cookable vegetables were often scarce in Iran, too, except for melons, which were an important crop and became a feature of our diet while we were there, as they had been to a lesser extent, in Turkey.

In spite of (or perhaps because of) the lack of exotic additions to a rather monotonous menu, we were remarkably free from any digestive upsets, and of course we were always very particular about not drinking any water that was not first boiled and then drunk in the form of tea.

On our first morning in Iran (then still often called 'Persia' by the British) we followed the road to the top of a steep range — the Pai Taq or 'Pass of the Hag' — and found ourselves on dry and apparently barren uplands, more than 3000 feet above sea level. We passed the small town of Kerend and continued to cross wide dry valleys and bare ridges without seeing many signs of a settled rural population.

There were, however, some indications of oil production in the area, with two pumping stations and a small refinery on the road just before we came to Kermanshah, which was the first large town that we saw in Iran. From then on there was rather more traffic, consisting mainly of tanker lorries belonging to the Anglo-Iranian Oil Company, a few small buses and the occasional car. The roads were generally quite wide and well laid out, but with gravel surfaces that were formed into terrible corrugations by the traffic, making rough going for the poor old Morris, which had neither the speed nor the weight to ride over them.

Just beyond Kermanshah, at Taq-e Bostan, we stopped to look at carvings high up on a rockface that depicted the conquests of some of the kings of ancient Persia, but somehow we missed seeing the more famous carvings at Bisitun a few miles further on. These describe in three different cuneiform languages (Persian, Babylonian and Median), cut into the rock in about 518 BC, the warlike achievements of King Darius 1, who was the leader of the invading Persian army that the Greeks eventually defeated at the battle of Marathon in 490 BC. It was these inscriptions that were deciphered in the 1840s by the archaeologist Rawlinson and others, and gave European scholars the key to the translation of those previously lost languages.

We were now high up on the plateau, and the morning was cold as we drove through Kangavar, climbing towards Hamadan, the ancient 'Ecbatana', which had been the capital of Cyrus the Great, conqueror and ruler of Asia from the Mediterranean to the Hindu Kush in the sixth century AD, and became the summer capital of Persian kings.

The valley near Kerend, Iran.

The road on the plateau near Kangavar.

UD4689

A village near Avej, Iran.

Hamadan is recorded in the logbook as being 6280 feet, or 2059 metres, above sea level, and the mountain called the Kuh-e Alvand, just south of the town, is shown on modern maps to be 3572 metres (11,787 feet) high. It was, and still is, an important road junction; connecting routes from the north-west out of Anatolia or southern Russia, the north from the Caspian coast and the east from Teheran, with the road from the south-west, which we had followed from Mesopotamia.

Ted, who travelled that way again in 1976, reports that there is now a modern highway crossing the pass leading over to Hamadan, directly on top of the line of the old road that we were on.

We were in Hamadan for about four hours, which gave us time to admire its wide streets, central square and cool atmosphere, but mainly to have the broken leaves in the front springs replaced, which from now on, because of the state of the roads, we seemed to have to do at almost every large town we came to. We carried complete spare front and rear springs with us, and soon we could change one nearly as quickly as we could a tyre, but replacing the broken leaves was a blacksmith's job and we found that the local tradesmen, having had a lot of practice, could do it very efficiently.

Desolate mountain ranges near Hamadan.

The road continued north-east from Hamadan over fairly level country with rough eroded hills on both sides of us. There was no sign of cultivation away from the floor of the valleys, and very little vegetation anywhere on the sides of the hills, so that the country gave the impression, as winter approached, of being almost completely arid. This was hard to reconcile with what we knew of the history of Iran, Anatolia and Mesopotamia; of the many great civilisations that had been nurtured in these places, and of the armies (such as Alexander's) that had marched for long distances over country that now seemed barely able to support a scattered population of peasants in a shepherding economy.

Certainly, as we soon began to realise, there must have been great changes to the climate of the vast area that we now know as the Middle East in the last two thousand years; changes that might yet be repeated in other climates, like our own. It was a sobering thought.

The road corrugations seemed to get worse as we went north-east from Hamadan and the old car shook alarmingly. Sure enough, the copper petrol pipe sprang a leak and we had continued trouble with other leaks around the filter, in spite of carefully mending them with our soldering iron.

After crossing another big range, we ran down to an area of wider valleys, again with some small-scale irrigation and a few villages of flat-roofed mud-brick houses along the road, which led us to the town of Avej.

It was near here that we first noticed mounds of earth running in long lines down the slopes from the foot of the mountains to the level ground. These mounds, we discovered, were the outward signs of the traditional irrigation system of Iran, the *qanats*. Each *qanat* consists of a series of shallow wells joined together underground by a tunnel to form a subterranean canal, which runs at a constant slope and carries water from snow-fed streams and springs in the mountains to be used for irrigation on the flats or to supply water to towns or villages. Apparently the tunnels can be as much as twenty-five miles long, but any that we saw would seem to have been very much less than that.

These tunnel systems have the great advantage that much less water is lost by evaporation from them than would be the case if it were carried in open channels, and because of this the *qanats* are still in use; I could see some examples from the air when approaching Isfahan in 1977. Nevertheless, they must be extraordinarily difficult and dangerous to build and maintain, and modern piping methods are now probably taking their place in the Iranian countryside.

A 'Persian' hound, similar in appearance to an afghan.

I noted in my diary this day that after Avej 'we went down a steep valley with red eroded hills and queer rock strata. Had lunch in open country under some trees by an irrigation channel and washed the car. A peasant came. I gave him some biscuits, whereupon he went and brought some beautiful grapes for us.'

We had been warned not to eat uncooked fruit or vegetables, especially those grown close to the soil (typhoid being endemic in the country), but we decided that grapes were probably clear on that count at least, and besides, they were too good to miss.

We were making more than a hundred miles a day now, in spite of the road corrugations. These made driving a misery on the worst sections, which seemed to grow longer and more frequent as the traffic increased closer to the capital. So far as we could see, there were no mechanical graders or other machinery in use on the roads and the only maintenance workers were small groups of disconsolate peasants, who seemed to be doing some kind of forced labour and had to rely on the simplest hand tools to help them to smooth out the irregularities in the road surface.

When we reached Kazvin, an attractive town some eighty miles north of Avej, we turned almost at right angles and ran south-east towards Teheran, skirting the foothills of the Elburz Mountains, which form a barrier between the main plateau and the Caspian Sea, and still making fair progress, in spite of having to do more soldering jobs on the petrol pipe now and then.

Then, after passing through Karaj (petrol and passports again) suddenly we saw, rising out of the haze ahead of us, a perfectly shaped snow-capped volcanic cone, glistening white where the sun shone on it and seeming to float above the flat horizon, unconnected with the ground.

We were not expecting such a sight, and looked at the map for clues to identify what seemed to be some kind of mirage. Soon we found it, clearly marked as Mt Demavand, 17,251 feet high (5601 metres), north-east of Teheran and sixty miles from where we were.

It seemed a good idea to stop and admire this unexpected vision and so, as we were both rather travel-stained and short of clean clothes, we made an early camp in the afternoon and did some washing to prepare ourselves for our entry to the capital.

While we were doing these chores, a young man approached the car, accompanied by several elegant dogs shaped like greyhounds but with long floppy ears and soft silky coats of the spaniel type. We took some photographs of these fine animals, though none of their owner, partly because we had been warned against taking pictures of people while in Iran on account of both official and religious sensitivities.

In general, the shah's policy was to encourage the image of Iran as being 'modern', so that pictures of anything that was new were allowable (but generally uninteresting), while subjects that we would have thought to be picturesque might turn out to be unacceptable to the authorities, which in practice meant the police. One consequence of this was that we were wary of taking photographs in the towns or villages, where the police were often in evidence.

Our camp between Avej and Teheran.

When we drove into Teheran the next morning we found that, true to our usual luck, both the post office and the banks were shut, it being a holiday of some kind. To our relief, however, the British Consulate did not observe it and we found that the consul, whose name was Summerhayes, was both helpful and hospitable, so much so that he invited us to come and stay with him and his wife in the legation compound.

For the rest of the morning we looked around Teheran, then probably less than a quarter of its present size and then, as now, not a particularly distinguished place. We did record seeing new university and airport buildings as we drove into town, but there seemed to be almost no ancient monuments nor splendid mosques, such as we might have expected to find.

In the bazaar we looked at some carpets — 'good but expensive' — which we did not buy, not only because of the price, but also because there was at that time a stiff export tax on them, payable at the frontier on leaving, which further discouraged us. In the end, feeling that I must take back at least one gift for my fiancée from Iran, I bought a small round ornamented box of Isfahan silver. Ted and I both had haircuts in a surprisingly Western-style barber shop and then returned to the consulate, where we were given a guide to take us to the British compound.

This was a beautiful leafy enclosure, situated behind high walls, in the tradition of the Persian walled garden, on a sunny slope at Gulhek, six miles north of the city. Here we were greeted by Mrs Summerhayes and given a comfortable room and a bath, followed by tea and then dinner.

The Summerhayes were not only kind hosts, they also told us a lot about Iran that was not included in the information given to us by any of the Iranian officials to whom we had spoken.

They described how the then reigning shah, Reza Pahlavi (father of the more recently deposed ruler of the same name), who had been an army officer of obscure origins and later Minister for War, had seized power and had himself appointed to be shah, not many years before. He had then set out to reduce the influence of the tribal chieftains, who had controlled most of the country in an almost feudal style and had previously maintained a great degree of independence from the central government.

At the same time he, like Ataturk, had sought to make social and religious changes, including raising the status of Iranian women by abolishing the use of the veil, or *chadour*, and 'modernising' the dress of the men by making them wear European clothes. These included what were called *Pahlavi* caps, rather like those that the Turks wore, with short stiff peaks, said to discourage the wearers from touching the ground with their foreheads when making their ritual obeisances towards Mecca. Most of these changes had been opposed by both the mullahs and the tribal chiefs.

In 1935, on the pretext of negotiating a settlement of some of the matters in dispute, especially as regards the exercise of power by the Teheran government, the shah had invited a number of the chieftains, with their followers and some of the leading mullahs, to a meeting with him in the courtyard of the Shrine of the Imam Reza, the holy place of the Shi'ite Moslems at Meshed, about 600 miles east of Teheran.

When the delegates were assembled in the courtyard, he had, ostensibly to quell a riot, ordered his troops to turn their machine-guns on the crowd and many were killed, thus reducing the strength of the opposition to his proposed reforms.

OCTOBER, 1938.

Monday 10

An entry from Owen's diary for Monday, 10 October 1938.

A youth wearing a Pahlavi cap near Avej, Iran.

Nevertheless, the shah still felt the need to be watchful for any possible new unrest in the country and that, combined with a general and long-established suspicion of all foreigners, gave the police great power to enforce their authority. We were warned against taking them and their seemingly trivial rules against photography and constant demands for passports, too lightly. It was also made clear to us that should we be 'picked-up' for breaches of these rules, it might be some time before the British authorities could arrange for our release. Therefore, we must take care not to offend Iranian officialdom if we wished to continue our trip without hindrance from them. In view of the constraints of our timetable and our tight financial position, we willingly promised to take this advice to heart, and to do our utmost to try to conform with the wishes of the constabulary, however unreasonable we might think they were.

The following morning, after a pleasant breakfast that included a bowl of *ma'ast*, a form of yoghurt made from mare's milk, we said our farewells to the Summerhayes and drove back into the city.

We went straight to police headquarters, chiefly to ask for the extension of our fourteen-day transit visas, which, we had been assured by the Iranian consulate in London, would be readily available to us once we got to Teheran. Needless to say, we were now told that we should go on to Meshed, where (they said) we would be readily given whatever extra time we required to travel through to the frontier.

Police permit issued in Iran, allowing us to proceed by an altered route, which we eventually did not use.

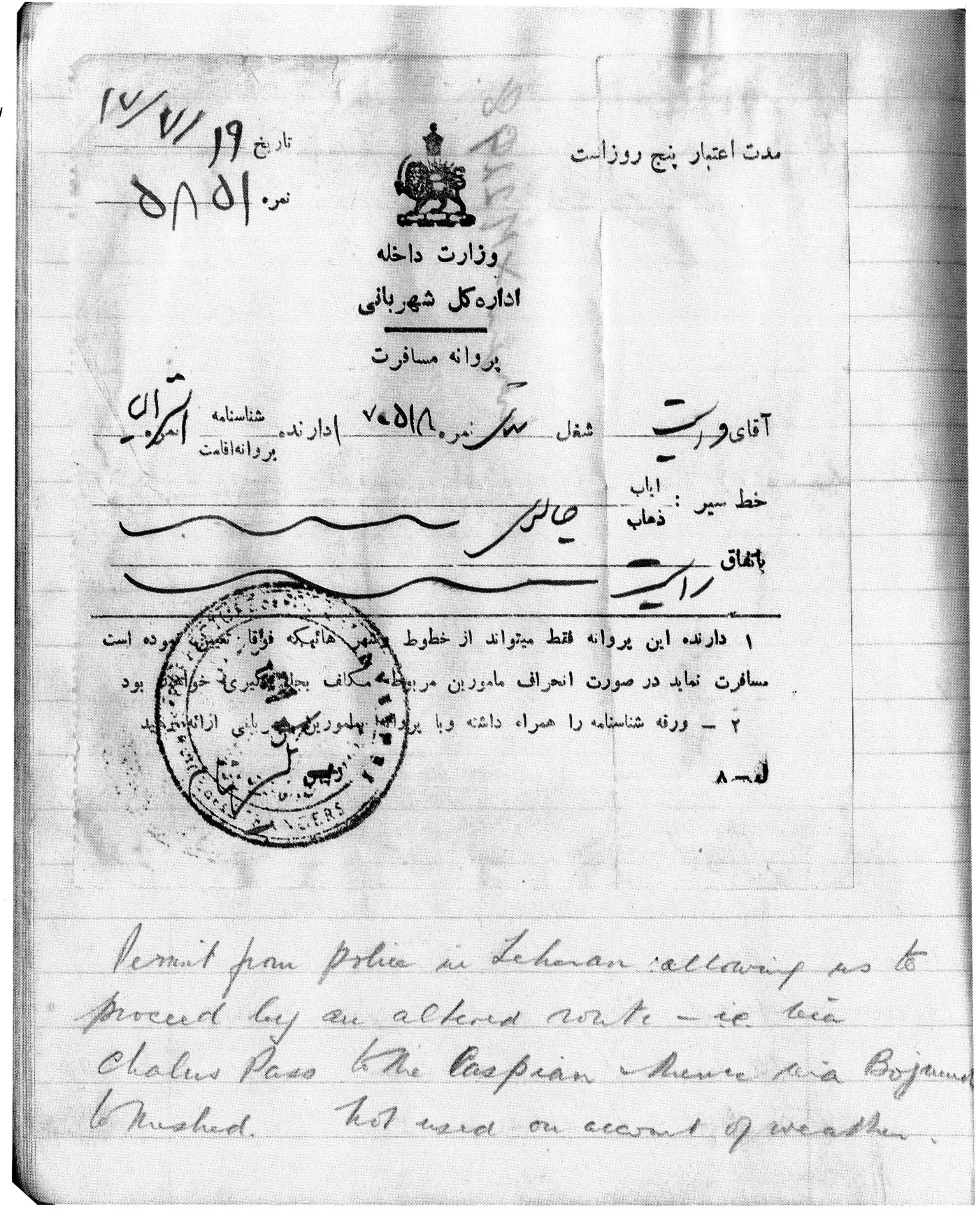

مدت اعتبار پنج روزاست

تاریخ ۱۷/۷/۱۹

نمره ۵۸۵۱

وزارت داخله

اداره کل شهربانی

پروانه مسافرت

آقای ... شغل ... دارنده شناسنامه / پروانه اقامت نمره ۷۰۵۱۸

خط سیر : ایاب / ذهاب

باتفاق

۱ دارنده این پروانه فقط میتواند از خطوط و شهرهائیکه فوقا تعیین شده است مسافرت نماید در صورت انحراف مامورین مربوطه مکلف بجلوگیری خواهند بود

۲ — ورقه شناسنامه را همراه داشته وبا پروانه بمامورین شهربانی ارائه دهید

ط ـ ۸

Permit from police in Teheran: allowing us to proceed by an altered route – i.e. via Chalus Pass to the Caspian thence via Bojnurd to Meshed. Not used on account of weather.

We reckoned we could easily enough get to Meshed within the week left to us before our time expired, so long as we could maintain our current average of about a hundred miles a day. Therefore we accepted the situation and even applied for, and were granted, permission to diverge from the direct route due east across the Iranian Plateau, and instead to go north for about seventy miles over the Elburz Range via the Chablus Pass to the Caspian Sea, then to travel east along the coastline, which, we heard, was warm, fertile and relatively moist.

This prospect sounded very tempting; we were becoming tired of constant travelling on dusty roads through semi-deserts and would have welcomed the sight of some green vegetation. However, after talking to the people at the Anglo-Iranian Oil Company's office, we were put off the idea, because of the risk of snow in the mountains and doubts about the state of the road around the eastern end of the Elburz through Bojnurd, which we would have had to follow on our way back south to Meshed.

Accordingly, we decided to stick to the direct route and so set out east from Teheran in the late afternoon towards Firuzkuh, along what must once have been the old Silk Road to China, and made camp about thirty miles from the city.

The next few days brought their share of trouble. Some distance along the road, after an early start, we found that we had two more broken leaves in one of the front springs, so we had to put in the spare one, and at the same time replace a loose rivet in the chassis at the point where one of the engine support brackets was secured to it, all of which took about three hours.

Then we struck a very strong, cold head wind as we crossed a series of ridges that ran down from the Elburz, and in so doing sustained another puncture, so that when we made camp in a dry gully, partly out of the wind, we felt we were lucky to have managed our hundred miles for that day.

The weather turned showery and cold during the night, and in the morning there was snow visible on the hills not far away, as we came out on to a bare plain to enter the town of Semnan.

Here again we went through the routine of leaving the damaged spring with a blacksmith, while we walked through the big covered bazaar, filled with a great variety of shops and stalls and with small workshops making such things as rag soles for sandals and flat metal shoes for donkeys. I bought one of these and still have it, hanging on the office wall, but I am bound to say that it did not bring us any immediate good luck.

The wind stayed blustery and cold as we left Semnan and climbed over another desolate range on to a desert plain. We were on a stretch of badly corrugated road when, about sundown, we turned off to the left towards the shelter of a rocky hill that rose out of the desert not far away from the road. The soil was quite soft at the base of the hill, which seemed to cause the car to move rather more sluggishly, until suddenly it stopped, apparently through loss of power to the back wheels. No amount of gear-changing nor engine-revving had any effect and we realised we were there to stay.

It was not a happy prospect that we contemplated as we sat in the car with the wind howling round us in violent gusts. We were by then about 200 miles out from Teheran, the only place we knew of where we could expect to find worthwhile help, and we were still 400 miles from our immediate destination at Meshed, while the frontier with British India was, by the route that we had decided to take, about another 700 further on.

Meantime our visas would expire in four days, leaving us at the mercy of the unsympathetic and not very literate provincial police.

Worst of all was the situation regarding the car itself. If, as then seemed likely, it could not be repaired well enough for us to be able to drive it away, we were, in the terms of the 'carnet' document under which we had brought it into Iran, responsible for seeing that it was taken out of the country again. Otherwise we would have to pay a hefty duty on its full value, no matter whether it could be salvaged or not.

Its true worth outside Iran would not have been much more than thirty or forty pounds sterling at the most, but because of the system of tariffs and other restrictions on trade that were in force within the country, the price would have been inflated far beyond its proper figure and we had heard alarming talk of the financial penalties that could be inflicted on those people unlucky enough to be caught in the position of having to abandon their vehicles without a customs clearance. Clearly the Iranians were not then in the business of trying to encourage tourists to travel in their country.

The weather was much too bad for us to investigate the cause of our unexpected stoppage that evening, so we settled down to endure an uncomfortable night, sitting up in the car with all our available clothes on and dozing until sunrise, when we found that the storm had cleared and taken with it the worst of our forebodings of the night before.

We soon discovered why we had suffered such a sudden loss of traction. The drive to the rear wheels was delivered through large flanges on the outboard ends of the axle half-shafts, on to which the wheel hubs were bolted. One of these flanges had sheared off the axle, so that the shaft could turn freely without transmitting any torque to the wheel.

This was a bad blow, but we soon realised that the damage could be repaired easily enough, if only we could get the axle to a workshop with the necessary equipment to weld the flange back on again — too much to expect of the average Iranian blacksmith of the period.

We also realised that, although we could see no signs of life as we surveyed the desolate scene around our camp, we were by no means alone in an uninhabited desert. Alongside us ran the only road between Teheran and Meshed and, because of the great religious importance of the latter, pilgrims went to and fro between the two cities in dilapidated buses. There were occasional trucks on the road as well.

Only one solution offered itself. We pulled out the half shaft and Ted, with it under his arm, eventually flagged down a passing bus and set off back to Teheran to enlist the help of the consulate in getting the shaft repaired and, just as importantly, in persuading the appropriate authorities to extend our visas to cover any delay in our arrival at Meshed.

Meanwhile, having waved him off with a show of cheerfulness that I did not really feel, I spent the rest of the day doing jobs around the camp and the next morning started to do some routine maintenance on the car. Lying on my back in the dusty soil, greasing and checking over the springs and steering linkages, I suddenly noticed that a large crack had opened up across the face of the main chassis member, just at the point where the engine mounting, which we had worked on the day before, was secured.

I stared at the crack unbelievingly. To me it seemed that a broken chassis member must spell absolute disaster as far as the car was concerned, and with it the end of our journey. Therefore my immediate problem became how to get in touch with Ted to tell

Disaster Camp, 400 miles from Meshed, Iran.

OCTOBER, 1938.

Friday 14

time again this morning.
Ted found that driving flange
on off side rear wheel hub
was broken & decided to
go to Teheran & try to get it
welded or else a new one
We stopped in v. crowded inn
& he left about 9.30 for
Samnan & thence Teheran
I stayed with the car & lay
about reading most of the
day feeling rather disconsolate.
Flat stony plain stretching
away beyond the road to the
east, ~~[struck out]~~ & south while to
the west & N. west (on our side
of the road) there are ranges
of high & v. rocky hills with
fresh snow showing on those
in front of us. Hot today but
cool again this evening no wind

OCTOBER, 1938.

Saturday 15

Started to mend radiator & front
petrol tank when I found a
serious crack in the offside main
chassis member where the engine
support bracket is attached.
Decided to go to Damghan & wire
Brit. Consul Tehran to get message to
Ted telling him car might be done
for in any case. Got lift to
D. in lorry arriving 12.30, met
by policeman as usual & finally
taken to chief of police where youth
interpreted in French. After
delay went to telephone but it
was shut till 3. Spent from
3 till 4 trying to get onto Teheran
without success so went back
to garage & got lift on heavy
truck back to car arriving
after dark. Driver inspected chassis
& said it could be repaired at Damghan

Entries from Owen's diary for 14–15 October 1938.

him not to bother about fixing the axle, because in any case the car was now virtually undriveable.

I knew I would have to get to a telephone to ring the consulate to explain what a fix we were in and to leave messages for Ted, assuming that he had reached Teheran, so as to let him know what had happened. Looking at the map it seemed that the nearest phone would most likely be at Damghan, the next town on the road ahead of us, only about twenty miles away.

Just before midday I picked up a lift on a lorry heading in that direction. When we stopped at the police post outside the town I was taken to the station to be questioned by the senior officer as to my business there. After some futile attempts on both sides to communicate with one another, a youth was produced who spoke some French, and through him I managed to convey to the officer the urgency of my position.

Finally I was allowed to go and was directed to the post office, which was shut for lunch until three o'clock. When it opened for business again, I found that the 'exchange' was in an upstairs room of the building and consisted of a single telephone attached to the wall in the charge of a rather scruffy-looking man with a companion who appeared to be a genuine albino, and who presumably had to spend the daylight hours indoors because of his condition.

In response to my calls of 'Telephone Teheran!' and 'British Consulate!' the operator would wind the ringing handle and say 'Allo, Allo' into the microphone that projected from the body of the instrument, while holding the receiver to his ear. No one ever answered him, but he continued to repeat the sequence on and off for about an hour until I reluctantly decided to give up and to look instead for a lift back to the car. I felt sure that if I did not get to the site in daylight I would never find it again.

It was getting late when I spotted the Morris, standing forlornly at the foot of the bare ridge in the desert landscape, but the truck driver who had given me the lift kindly came over to look at the damage with me and indicated that in his opinion the crack could be repaired, even in Damghan. This was a great relief and it was an even greater one when soon afterwards Ted turned up, almost in the dark, with the repaired axle, having been lucky enough to find a cotton mill run by some Germans at Semnan, who had welded the severed parts together again.

Ted later wrote a vivid account of his journey in a letter to his family:

> There are a lot of buses on this road taking pilgrims to and from Meshed; which is second only to Mecca as a holy place for the Shias; so I boarded the first of these buses going towards Teheran. It turned out to be a bad bus and it broke down all the time. The pilgrims were very kind and at once gave me sweets and nuts to eat and one even wanted to give me his seat (I sat on a tool box near the driver).
>
> The Persian has a good sense of humour and we had great jokes all day. When we stopped for lunch at a tea house I had my lunch with three others and ate an enormous feed of rice, meat curry, sour milk, slabs of Persian bread and glasses of very sweet tea without milk.
>
> At this lunch stop the driver and the mechanic tinkered with various parts for four hours, so we drank innumerable glasses of tea. Finally we went off again to cries of 'Allah! Mohammed! and Ali!' Sometimes the bus just got over a hill to

> shouts of triumph from the pilgrims; at other times it stopped and the mechanic would get out and put stones behind the wheels, until the engine had cooled off. At the last hill he got his hand caught under the back wheel and tore the flesh of three fingers badly.
>
> I tied it up with one of your last Christmas handkerchiefs, which was no doubt the only clean thing in the bus. The driver then made all haste for Semnan and a doctor. Fortunately this was the last hill and for the rest of the way the road was over a plain and had no bends, so the all-out speed of the bus was not so alarming. Before long these efforts had boiled the radiator dry and the engine stopped. This meant a delay of about a quarter of an hour while the engine cooled off. We got to Semnan about 7.30 p.m., having taken since 9.30 a.m. to do about 55 miles.

Later, Ted told me how he had stayed the night at an hotel in Semnan, sharing a large room with about a dozen others, the toilet facilities being a deep hole in the floor. But in spite of this inconvenience and the lack of privacy, he had enjoyed his excursion.

We had some trouble replacing the axle next morning, but in the end were able to drive, very cautiously because of the cracked chassis, to Damghan by mid-day. The local blacksmith was a slow starter and it was nearly five o'clock before he and his boy assistants really began work on the job.

Meanwhile we repaired the radiator ourselves and refitted the half shaft by reaming out the holes in the flange. The blacksmith and his gang made a plate to bolt over the crack and had it ready to fit by ten o'clock that night, when they began to show signs of wanting to stop work, making pathetic gestures of fatigue. It needed great persuasive powers on our part to induce them to finish the job by replacing the mudguard and running board again; but in the end they did it, and we were back on the road soon after midnight, and slowly drove the forty miles to the small town of Sharud, where we pulled up for a short rest at four in the morning.

By now we realised that we would have to modify our style of driving greatly if we were to have any chance of getting the car to Meshed on its own wheels, while at the same time we had the problem of catching up two lost days, so as to keep within the time limit of our visas. We decided to reduce our speed to about fifteen miles per hour so that the car's wheels would roll in and out of the corrugations, like a small boat in a heavy swell, instead of bumping from crest to crest. To make up for the lower speed of travel, we would have to drive almost non-stop, and this we set out to do when we started from Sharud before sunrise.

Unfortunately, the new plate on the chassis was a fairly rough fit and it soon worked loose. The resultant movement in the frame of the car caused the radiator leak to open up again, so that it had to be re-soldered and the plate tightened in mid-morning. From then on we managed to keep moving almost continuously, so that by seven the next morning we were near Nishapur, about 240 miles east of Sharud and only eighty miles from Meshed, on the very day that our visas were due to run out.

We were delighted to be at Nishapur after such a long an uncomfortable night's driving. Not only was it the birthplace of the poet Omar Khayyam and hence a town of interest and romance, but we also felt that now we had time to complete the last short lap to Meshed at our leisure, when the worries and troubles of the last few days would

17/10/38 (cont) Mon)

6.30	Stopped for breakfast.	
10.30–1.15	Stopped to mend radiator & tighten up plate on side member. Very hot sun — had lunch. Changed the oil.	5657
4.30–40	Affasabad — petrol found —	5701
5–6 pm	Stopped for a meal & then drove on	5704
11.45 pm	Sabzawar — petrol, "cheque", passports OK	5776

18/10/38

7–7.45	Nishapore — held up by police re passports — Omar Khayyam etc	5850
8–8.45	Breakfast & clean up.	
9.20	5000 miles out from London	5866
10.45	Passed road junction at Sharifabad	5895
2.30	Arrived Meshed — very bad road for last 30 miles. Went to police & British Consulate.	5937

Entries from the logbook for 17–18 October 1938.

surely be over and we would arrive triumphant at Police Headquarters there, with time to spare.

It did not turn out that way. When we reported to the police post on the outskirts of Nishapur, it soon became apparent that something was wrong. We were not allowed to go on, and I was escorted to an upstairs room at the main station while Ted stayed below to mind the car. Gradually I understood the problem, which was that by our reckoning the visas, due to expire that day, should be valid until midnight, but by the Iranian count they had expired just after midnight on the night before.

I did my best to argue about it, but with little success. To settle the matter the sergeant telephoned the local chief of police and when that official answered he handed me the receiver.

I said, 'Hullo, do you speak English?' as confidently as I could.

No answer.

'Parlez-vous Francais?'; whereupon a harsh voice replied, 'Der Deutsch ich spreche.'

I quickly answered 'Nein spreche der Deutsch', which was about the extent of my knowledge of German phrases, and gave the receiver back to the sergeant. He seemed then to get a burst from his superior at the other end of the line, but nevertheless proceeded to give me a breakfast of some *chai* and flat bread, while we waited for the officer to arrive.

When he came, he was obviously annoyed at having been disturbed so early, but took most of his ill-humour out on the unfortunate sergeant. Finally, after some further talk between themselves, they decided to ring headquarters at Meshed and then soon afterwards handed back our passports and sent us on our way.

The road surface on the last lap of our journey to Meshed seemed to be even worse than usual, but we finally made it to the British consulate in the mid-afternoon, and saw the consul-general (Meshed, because of its proximity to Russia, Afghanistan and India was an important post), who sent his Iranian clerk with us to interview the city's chief of police.

The latter was an imposing figure, sitting behind a big desk in his large office and

Iranian bank note.

obviously enjoying the situation of having two British subjects, and European at that, petitioning him for a favour.

We first of all had to state our case and make a request for an extension of time, in written French. This letter took us a while to prepare ('Nous sommes deux voyageurs anglais') and in it we asked for a ten-day extension to our visas so as to have a little time to spare on the road and to be free of the worries of the past week. The chief took the paper, read it, made some corrections to the grammar and indicated that he would be only too happy to do whatever we might wish. He then called a clerk, threw the passports across the room at him, and ordered glasses of *chai* to be brought in.

While we sipped the hot sweet tea, we conversed (still in French, of course) about Iran and what a fine place it was, and the people also etcetera etcetera, until the clerk returned with our passports, which the chief then examined, signed with a great flourish and handed back to us with a bow, indicating the end of the interview.

We left the room with great expressions of cordiality on both sides, however, when we were outside the building we looked at the passports and found that we had been given only five days to get out of the country.

It was obviously no use going back to complain; the language problem alone gave the chief far too much scope for not understanding why we should need more time. So we returned to the British compound, where Mr and Mrs Hart, the vice-consul and his wife, had kindly offered us accommodation.

We were invited to dinner that night at the house of the consul-general, whose name was Squires, and where the guest of honour was the Afghan consul-general, a distinguished looking old gentleman with a neatly trimmed beard and a bald head, whose only second language was French (the 'language of diplomacy'), which rather restricted the conversation during dinner.

In deference to him we played an after-dinner game that did not require much spoken participation by the players. It was called *ulah* or 'donkey' and it involved people sitting round a table each holding a piece of string tied to a cork, with all the corks grouped together in the centre of the table. At a given signal, which somehow depended on the throw of dice, one player would try to catch as many of the other players' corks as possible, using an inverted round Gold Flake cigarette tin to trap them before they could be pulled away. It was quite a hilarious game. I don't remember who (if anybody) won, but I'm sure that Ted and I were too tired to care, after our non-stop driving efforts of the past thirty-six hours.

Next day we took the car to a garage run by an Indian who replaced the Damghan plate, which had itself cracked, with a new one and also fitted stays to the radiator to hold it steady. Since the original crack had developed, there had been some subsidence in the chassis, so that we could not fit the bonnet into the space between the firewall and the top of the radiator to support the latter, and had in fact taken to carrying the bonnet inside the car, on top of all our other gear.

While the repairs were being done on the Morris, we walked along the road that ran round the outside of the great mosque dedicated to the Imam Reza, having been warned by the consulate not to go inside for fear of causing trouble by our presence among the crowd of pilgrims in the shrine's courtyard. There, only three years before, the shah's troops had been involved in the notorious massacre.

I commented in my diary that 'the present shah is out to break the power of the mullahs', and it is strange to think that this was written just forty years before the mullah Khomeini broke the power of the old shah's son.

Instead of seeing the inside of the famous mosque (which I have always wished we could have done) we went to the bazaar where Ted bought a *poshteen*, a full-length sheepskin coat embroidered with raw silk — very smart, but almost too warm for Australian conditions.

The Indian mechanics did slow work on the car, which was not finished until the following day, and it was three in the afternoon when we said goodbye to the Squires and the Harts, who had been so kind to us, and set off on yet another race against time, with only four days left to get to the border with British Baluchistan, near Zahedan, due west of Quetta.

We began to regret that we had decided to accept the advice, given to us in London, against going through Afghanistan. A more direct route than the one we took, and certainly a more interesting one, would have been to travel from Meshed south-east into Afghanistan, through Herat to Kandahar and either to continue thence south-east to Quetta, or else to go north-east to Kabul and then into India via the Khyber Pass.

According to the people at the consulate in Meshed, it might still have been feasible to do either; provided that the local Afghan consulate would provide visas for us. However, because of the short time left on our Iranian visas and the general feeling of pressure to get back on the road again, we decided not to try to arrange entry into Afghanistan, but to stick to the original plan, even though we realised that in the long run this might add extra time and distance to our journey.

It also meant that we had to begin this leg of the trip with another tiring all-night drive southward, though strangely enough the road improved as we got further from Meshed and the traffic volume dropped almost to zero. However the road consequently became more difficult to find and at sometime around midnight, after passing through the small town of Torbat, we began to feel uncertain about our course and so decided to consult our little compass (for the first time on the trip) to check on the general direction of the road we were following.

The compass card, wobbling uncertainly in the headlights, told us that we were in fact going south-east instead of due south, but we chose not to believe the reading, and kept on following the same track until, after talking to a very sleepy policeman in the small hours of the morning, we found that we were indeed off course. There was nothing for it but to go back forty-odd miles on our tracks, almost to Torbat, and then to turn due south again towards Birjand, where we did not arrive until ten the next night, after a wearying non-stop stage of about 400 miles from Meshed.

There was a British vice-consulate in Birjand, to which we were directed, and we managed to arouse the Indian clerk, who gave us a room to sleep in and some tea. By this time we were both suffering from colds and feeling generally rather sick, so we lay in for a while in the morning and left again about 10.30. We stopped for a late lunch near the small village of Shusp, with some areas of irrigation nearby, and while we were boiling up our billy, we were visited by two young men dressed in pre-Pahlevi style baggy white trousers and head cloths instead of caps. They gave us some raw carrots to add to our dry rations and were photographed without showing the least sign of concern.

Enjoying the company of locals over a lunch of raw carrots near Shusp.

Our Morris, more or less in one piece, near Zahedan.

The road continued to be 'fair' through Shusp and Quiemabad and at the latter place we filled up with petrol and some extra water late in the afternoon, ready to take on the desert stage of 190 miles to Zahedan.

After driving on for an hour at the end of the day, we made camp in the open before dark, but were on the road again about 1.30 the next morning and took turns to drive until daylight. We stopped for breakfast on a low stony ridge, as the sun was rising over a horizon of sandhills, a scene that produced in us an extraordinarily strong illusion that we were looking out over the sea.

Then we found that the main leaf in one front spring had gone yet again, and that a smaller leaf was broken in the other one. We had no sound spare left, so we packed the worst spring up with a wooden block, which we carried for such emergencies, and drove slowly over a rugged range of hills, soon afterwards passing a big black rock called the 'Kuh-e Malek Siah' where Iran, Afghanistan and Baluchistan adjoin.

We stopped for lunch in sight of Zahedan. It was very hot by then and the road, now very rough again, ran through desolate rocky hills. 'Zahedan (the logbook says) lies in an open desert valley, surrounded by low hills of crumbling black rock.' It was some distance from the actual frontier with British Baluchistan at Mirjawa, and again there was a vice-consulate in the town , also under the temporary charge of an Indian clerk. He was a Moslem from the north of the country, dressed in a long buttoned-up coat and a turban, who said his name was 'Khan Sahib', which sounded more like a title than a name. He was very hospitable, in a reserved and official way, and he gave us a place inside the walls of the small dusty compound around the modest mud-brick consulate to put up our tent, and then directed us to another Indian garage, where we took the car for more spring repairs. He followed all this up by providing us with a good supper of hot Indian curry, washed down by cups (not glasses any more) of tea, now with milk added to it in the Indian style.

Furthermore, the next day he arranged to have a supply of petrol sent on to Nok Kundi for us and said that we could pay for it, and the spring repairs, there in Iranian *rials* at the 'black' rate of 140 *rials* to the pound sterling, instead of the official 80.

Nok Kundi was a village nearly a hundred miles inside the Baluchistan border and the terminus of the railway line from Quetta, 300 miles further east. During the First World War this line had been extended over into Iran as far as Zahedan, but since then a section on either side of the border had been closed (perhaps it didn't pay!) and the rails removed, leaving the sleepers half covered by sand.

The next morning was divided between resting, doing our washing and visiting the garage where the car was being made roadworthy again.

Khan Sahib continued his very helpful efforts by giving us an excellent lunch of rice, fried chapatties and melon, and showing us his fine collection of rugs, before bidding us a dignified farewell.

It was four o'clock in the afternoon when we left Zahedan to drive the sixty miles to the frontier at Mirjawa, following the disused railway line. When we arrived at the Iranian post there, we were told that we would have to wait until next morning before we could go through their customs, so we pitched our tent in an abandoned 'garden' alongside the old railway station, near a pile of discarded sleepers, which we recognised as having been cut from Australian hardwood.

Customs clearance near the Iranian frontier, Mirjawa, 25 October 1938.

Mirjawa 25/10/38

نسخه اول

برای فروشنده ارز

بانک شاهنشاهی ایران
شعبه

بتاریخ ۱۳۱۷٫۷٫۱۹
شماره ۵۰/۹۱۱
ارز خریداری شده .... بارز
(بعدد) .... بریال
مبداء ارز ....

گواهینامه خرید ارزهای غیر صادراتی

بانک شاهنشاهی ایران (بانک مجاز) شعبه .... تصدیق مینماید که:
آقای/بنگاه .... مبلغ .... (بحروف) ارز خارجی که از قرار مظنه .... ریال
معادل .... (بحروف) ریال میشود بوسیله:
۱ ـ چک .... (صادر کننده چک) شماره .... مورخه ۱۷/۷/۱۹
عهدهٔ ....
۲ ـ حواله تلگرافی/کتبی از طرف .... مقیم .... توسط بانک ....
۳ ـ برات شماره .... مورخه .... بامضاء .... عهده
مقیم .... بموعد ....
۴ ـ
۵ ـ
در تاریخ ۱۷/۷/۱۹ باین بانک شاهنشاهی ایران بابت ....
بحساب کمیسیون ارز فروخته است:

بانک برای بانک شاهنشاهی ایران
شعبه رئیس حسابداری

نمونه شمارهٔ ۱۵۹
۱۰۰ کاره ۱۰۰ ورقی ۱۷٫۲٫۱۸

Up early in the morning, and checking over the car again as we were about to drive to the frontier post, we were dismayed to find that another crack had appeared in the chassis in the same position as the first one, but on the other side of the car.

We decided that we should cross the border into British territory at all costs, before attempting to do any repairs, and so, after clearing the Iranian customs with less than the expected fuss, we drove slowly but steadfastly down the road to the Indian post, which was shown on the map under the name of Killa Sufaid, and which consisted of a small mud-brick fort, manned by a single Sikh policeman.

With the representative of the British Raj, a Sikh warrant officer, at Killa Sufaid.

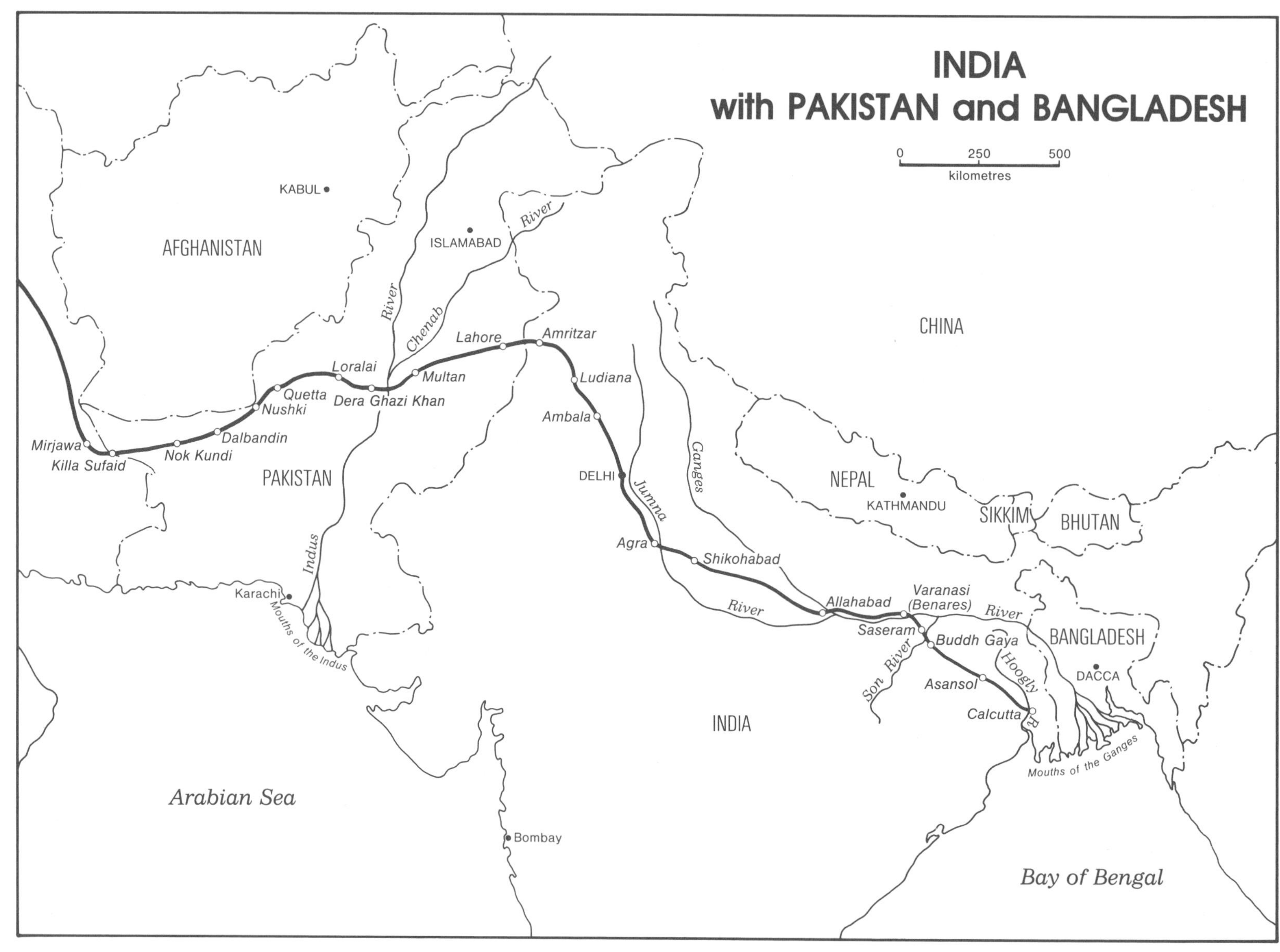
INDIA
with PAKISTAN and BANGLADESH
0
250
500
kilometres
KABUL
AFGHANISTAN
ISLAMABAD
River
River
Chenab
Lahore
Amritzar
Loralai
Multan
Ludiana
Quetta
Nushki
Dera Ghazi Khan
Ambala
Dalbandin
Mirjawa
Killa Sufaid
Nok Kundi
PAKISTAN
DELHI
Jumna
Ganges
NEPAL
KATHMANDU
SIKKIM
BHUTAN
CHINA
Indus
Agra
Shikohabad
Karachi
Mouths of the Indus
River
Allahabad
Varanasi
(Benares)
River
Saseram
Buddh Gaya
BANGLADESH
Son River
Hoogly
R.
Asansol
DACCA
Calcutta
INDIA
Mouths of the Ganges
Arabian Sea
Bombay
Bay of Bengal

4

INDIA

The little fort at Killa Sufaid was not an impressive sight in itself, but for us it was important as a sign that henceforth we would be coming under the influence and protection of the British Raj, something that we had often looked forward to when we were dealing with the more exasperating members of the Iranian police force.

The fort was a square building, whose sides were about sixty feet long and its thick walls nearly twenty feet high. The wall itself was pierced by a row of narrow slits that ran right around it a few feet from the top, designed to give defending riflemen, standing on a platform inside the building, an all-round field of fire, while themselves having some protection against the bullets of a possible enemy. There were square towers at each corner of the fort and a high gateway in the centre of one of the walls, with some sets of ibex horns mounted above it.

The fort at Killa Sufaid.

The Sikh warrant officer who commanded there was smartly dressed in a khaki drill tunic, with a Sam Brown belt, shorts and puttees and seemed to be the only 'regular' at the post. His attitude towards us was dignified and correct rather than cordial, but in our eyes he stood as a symbol of a stable and predictable system, which would be a great contrast to that which we had experienced during the previous three weeks.

Indeed, the time that we had spent in Iran seemed to be something of a nightmare as we looked back on it. Chiefly this was because of the atmosphere of uncertainty, and even of harassment, that we felt there, brought about by having to report to the police (generally twice) at nearly every town we passed through, and never being sure what their attitude towards us might turn out to be.

On top of this, the strain of driving for long distances over bad roads, so as to catch up time to avoid possible detention along the way, was making us very tired. And there was the worry that we might not succeed in getting out of the country before the car suffered some permanent disablement, which might force us to abandon it in the sparsely inhabited deserts of eastern Iran.

Now that we were in India, we felt that at least we were in friendly territory, so that help of some kind would be forthcoming if we needed it, while if the worst did happen and we had to walk away from the Morris, we would not have to pay an exhorbitant price for the privilege.

It seemed that others might have had the same feeling as they came to Killa Sufaid, because there were the wrecks of some old cars or trucks lying in the sand not far from

A street scene, Nok Kundi.

the fort, as though their owners had dragged them over the frontier before having to abandon them there.

We were not yet in that desperate situation, in spite of the threatening appearance of the new crack in the chassis, because we were still carrying the old Damghan plate, which had been replaced at Meshed, and we soon set to work to make use of it.

Our friend the Sikh policeman produced a couple of Baluchi companions and with their help we stripped down the left-hand side of the car. Then, by putting the plate on back-to-front, because the crack was on the opposite side to that for which the plate had been made, the holes in it again matched up with the rivet holes in the chassis.

When we had finished securing the plate, which took most of the day, the car was at least temporarily roadworthy again, so at about five in the afternoon we took photographs of the Outpost of Empire that was Killa Sufaid, and of the Sikh and his offsiders, and set out to drive cautiously towards Nok Kundi, still following the formation of the old railway line. About ten o'clock that night we made camp and, after an early start, arrived in mid-morning at Nok Kundi, where we went through the formalities of Indian Customs.

There was a weekly train between Nok Kundi and Quetta, which was due to go out the next day and, because of the uncertain state of the Morris and the uninhabited nature of much of the country ahead of us, we were inclined to swallow our pride and put the car on the train for that section of the journey.

However, the station master declared that we would have to wait until the following week for a suitable truck to be attached to the train at Quetta, so once again we resorted to the skills of the local blacksmiths and left the car for them to make up a fresh plate as a replacement for the old one from Damghan, while we looked around the town.

Nok Kundi was very much a frontier village, standing in open desert country, with a short main street of mud-brick huts in front of which stood one or two old lorrys and not much else. It did however have considerable importance as the terminus of the only railway in Baluchistan, because from there camel caravans travelled north into Afghanistan or south across the area marked on our map as the 'Sandy Desert', towards the Arabian Sea coast.

On the outskirts of the town, groups of Baluchis with big white turbans and fierce-looking beards sat about amongst their camels, the movements of their caravans dependent on those of the train. Apart from bringing in supplies from Quetta, it also brought the water for Nok Kundi from Dalbandin, a station about a hundred miles up the line, in what seemed to be a very small tender to carry a whole week's supply for a village.

After some enquiry, we found a room for the night in the village rest house, or *dak* bungalow. These places were a feature of most of the smaller Indian towns, being set up by the government to provide overnight accommodation for travellers; usually government officials and in those days probably always European, doing their rounds in the course of duty. We never enquired just what qualifications were needed to be able to use the bungalows, but no doubt being European, or more exactly British, would have been the main one. We went to them as a matter of course, without any pretence of being officials.

They varied in degrees of comfort, partly according to the size of the town they served, but also depending on the disposition of the Indian in charge, whose title was the *chowkidar*. Often they seemed to consist of only one or two rooms, provided with light wooden beds called *charpoys*, which used criss-crossed strips of webbing in place of mattresses; along with some chairs and a table, but very little else.

Two members of the Baluchi caravan, packing, Nok Kundi.

Firewood supplies, Nok Kundi.

A view of Nok Kundi village from the railway siding.

A camel patrol, armed with 303s, along the old railway line near the Iran/Baluchistan border.

Above: The water supply at Nok Kundi.

Left: Baluchis waiting with their caravan for the train, Nok Kundi.

In the foothills of the Ras Koh.

There was not much provision for the supply of food either, although the *chowkidar* would sometimes provide some rice and perhaps a curried chicken, as well as tea and flat bread (*chappati* in India) on demand.

The bungalows were a great boon to us because they were cheap and clean and, by our standards, quite comfortable. Besides, we soon discovered, when we moved into the more densely populated parts of India, that camping out there was much less feasible than it had been in the semi-desert country further west.

Accommodation was evidently limited in the *dak* bungalow at Nok Kundi; I noted in my diary that we had to move out after the first night because the room was needed for an official. We spent the second night of our stay in the waiting-room of the railway station, by courtesy of the station master, a Hindu who became quite a friend and gave us another welcome meal of Indian curry that evening.

The new plate for the car was not satisfactorily fitted into position until late on the second day, and in the meantime we did some shopping for food to carry us over the next two-day stage to Nushki, a drive during which we would see very little habitation except for one or two small sidings along the railway. It was against this eventuality that we had arranged for extra petrol to be delivered to Nok Kundi and so we filled our tanks, from four-gallon tins, to their capacity and made sure that we had some extra water as well.

The main event of that afternoon was the departure of the train for Quetta, at which most of the population of the village was present. The train consisted almost entirely of passenger carriages, with very little provision for freight, which was only to be expected when one considered the desolate nature of the countryside and the consequent lack of produce from it. However, there seemed to be plenty of would-be travellers, and one poor man was thrown off the train by the guard on to the ground (there was no platform), where he lay sobbing, whether from disappointment or actual injury we could not tell.

Next morning we were given breakfast by the station master, before we started off up the railway across a gibber desert of shiny black stones that must have been blisteringly hot in the summer. We passed the expected unmanned sidings and saw a few Baluchi fettlers working unenthusiatically on the permanent way, but otherwise there was no sign of any life.

Before dark we came to Dalbandin, which turned out to be quite an established village, as well as a watering point for the locomotives on the line, the water evidently coming from some underground source. We camped a few miles further along the track on a big clay-pan intersected by some small sandhills with patches of stunted bushes growing on them. Just to the north of us were the sombre black rocks of the Chagai Hills, which rose to a considerable height and formed the frontier with Afghanistan; while to the south were other steep ridges of black rock, the foothills of the Ras Koh, a parallel range whose highest point, according to the map, was about 10,000 feet.

The clay-pans continued to give us good travelling conditions, 'the best since Khanaqin' as the logbook describes them. At one stage the road went south towards the Ras Koh and we 'came to patches of rough grass with camels and goats grazing on them and encampments of Baluchis. The women and young girls mostly dressed in red saris and the men with large white head cloths wound round under their chins.'

That afternoon we reached the little town of Nushki, where there was a large walled

On the black gibber desert near Dalbandin.

Tribesmen between Dalbandin and Nushki.

compound with defensive towers at each of its corners. Here again we stayed in comfort at the *dak* bungalow.

There was petrol available at Nushki, so we replenished our supply and drove on towards Quetta through rocky hills on an improving road surface, which finally became bitumen after we passed the junction with the road that led south to Kalat. Kalat had once been the capital of Baluchistan, under a tribal khan, before the British took that country over towards the end of the nineteenth century and developed Quetta as the chief city, making it the rail junction for lines running north or west towards the Afghan border and connecting with the main Indian system to the east.

We ate an early lunch at the crossroads and saw a succession of Baluchi family groups leading pack camels or oxen, loaded with all their worldly possessions, and apparently heading south for winter quarters in the slightly more temperate climate of Kalat. We photographed some of these travellers and also the signpost saying 'London 5877 miles' — remarking that this was the first we had seen with that name on it since Dover.

Quetta had been devastated by an earthquake in 1935, and those parts of the town that had been re-built since then consisted mostly of asbestos sheeting and galvanised iron, which gave the whole place a very unattractive appearance. Still, the 'Quetta Hotel and Dak Bungalow', as it was described on the bill, was quite comfortable and provided us with a good dinner in more or less Western style, the landlady being English.

In the morning we called first of all on the Political Agent, a British official who was an influential figure in those parts, acting as a kind of liaison officer with the tribesmen. He gave us some information about the road ahead and also on the security situation, which, we gathered, would become rather uncertain after we passed Loralai, a day's drive further on.

Hotel and dak *bungalow, Quetta.*

Ted at Nushki.

Our bill from the Quetta Hotel and dak *bungalow.*

No. 326 Dated, 1. 11 1938

Mr Wright & Mr Whit Room No. 1 Dr.

Quetta Hotel & Dak Bungalow, QUETTA.

Cr.

Month & date.	Particulars.	Amount. Rs.	a.	p.	Remarks.
30 10/38	Board & Lodging	12	-	-	for 2 at [illegible]
31 10/38	do do	12	-	-	
1 11/38	Left after Break[illegible]				
		24	-	-	
	Total Rs. ...				

E. & O. E.

Received with thanks.

K. Thomas (Mrs)

Curzon Press, Quetta.

Quetta Hotel & Dak Bungalow, Quetta.

A Baluchi caravan on the Kalat road.

As far as we could understand, the problem was a local one of nomad banditry on a small scale, without much political significance. Just the same, there were risks involved and we were told to consult the military at Loralai before venturing on to the next stretch of road.

After this sobering chat, we went to the bazaar, where I bought a sheepskin waistcoat in the same style as the *poshteen* that Ted had purchased in Meshed, and also two small prayer rugs, one a Turcoman pattern and one a Turbat design, both made at Turbat in the south of Baluchistan. They were very cheap — fourteen rupees or about a pound sterling each — and are still in use in our family.

In the meantime we had called on the Morris agents, who were Indians and who took the car, washed and greased it and returned it on the promise that we would be photographed together with them before we left in the morning. This was done, but we never saw the results. They were noteworthy as being the only representatives of that then large company who showed any interest in us or our trip (apart from some correspondence in London before we left), which we thought might well have had some publicity value for Morris cars.

We drove north-east from Quetta, climbing over a pass at about 7500 feet and skirting round mountains that were much higher. Then we turned southward through Ziarat, noting that the stunted cypresses on the surrounding hills were the first natural timber we had seen since leaving the Taurus Mountains.

Loralai, our next stop, was a garrison town and in accordance with the instructions of the Political Agent in Quetta, we sent, via a 'sweeper' from the *dak* bungalow, a polite note to the Staff Captain requesting some information about the rules relating to travel on the next day's stage.

That section of the road, which we expected would take us out of the hills and down on to the Indus Plain at Dera Ghazi Khan, was supposed to be patrolled by troops from Loralai to protect travellers against 'bandits'.

He sent back a rather curt reply to the effect that we could only travel between eight am and six pm (it was during these hours that the road was meant to be guarded) and added that 'one member of the party, other than the driver, must be armed'.

Of course we had no arms of any kind with us, and would not have fancied our chances against a few determined tribesmen if we had had them, so there was nothing for it but to go on and hope for the best.

In the event we saw neither patrols nor tribesmen, except for another family group, evidently Pathan, consisting of one man, two women and several children with five or six Brahman-type cattle carrying their baggage, which included a few dead tree branches — their precious stock of firewood.

The husband or father of the party also had, slung on his shoulder, what appeared to be a genuine tribal-made Pathan rifle of very large bore and greatly ornamented about the stock, which he showed us with pride, but did not trust us to handle. I used to doubt whether these native-made firearms, of which one used to hear a good deal, really had a tribal origin, but some twenty years later Ted was shown over a small factory further

Above: The head of the family with his Pathan rifle.

Right: A Nomad family caravan near Rakni.

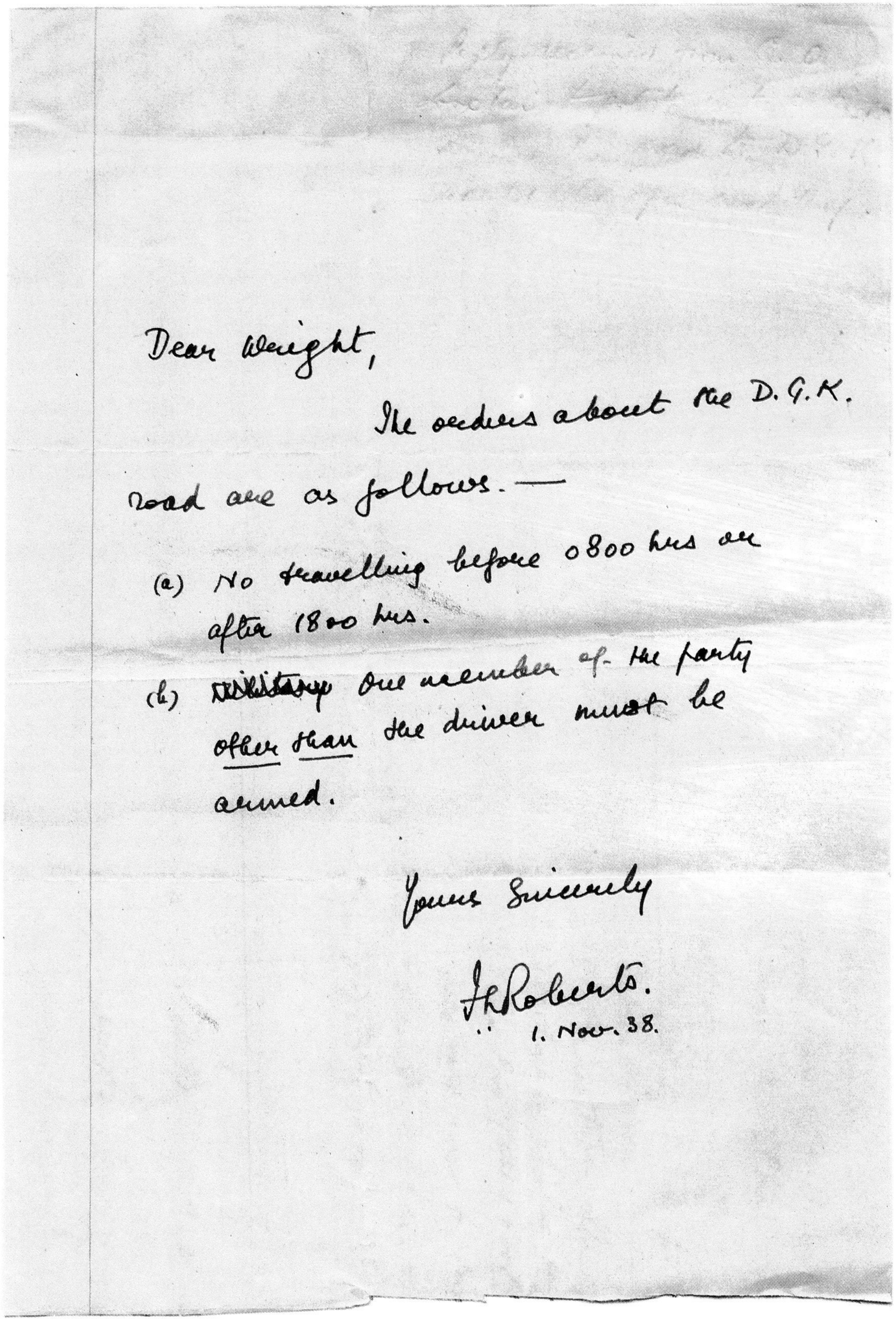

Dear Wright,

The orders about the D.G.K. road are as follows.—

(a) No travelling before 0800 hrs or after 1800 hrs.

(b) One member of the party other than the driver must be armed.

Yours Sincerely

J.L. Roberts.

1. Nov. 38.

Staff Captain's orders re travel to Dera Ghazi Khan.

north, near Peshawur, where weapons like this one were being made with very simple machinery.

Our meeting with the little caravan took place near Rakni, where there was a chain across the road to stop traffic going back into the 'bad country' late in the day. After that we climbed one more range of about 5000 feet up to Fort Munro, and then ran down a spectacular mountain road on to the flood plain of the great Indus River, only twenty miles of easy travelling from 'DGK', as it was universally called.

We did not fully realise it then, but we had now put behind us all the most difficult part of our trip, certainly as regards the kind of terrain that we would have to cross. There were still about 1700 miles to go before we reached Calcutta, however, almost all of that distance was over level ground and on reasonably good roads. Whatever troubles or delays we were to encounter from then on were mostly due to the great press of humanity on the roads and in the towns and villages, which set India apart from any other country that either of us had ever seen.

Dera Ghazi Khan was on the western side (you could hardly call such a flat area a 'bank') of the Indus and, when we left the local *dak* bungalow on a hot sunny morning, we went directly east across the sandy flood plain, with beds of tall reeds on either side of the road.

We crossed several wide, shallow channels by way of bridges formed from boats lashed together under a narrow wooden deck, covered with layers of reeds. The decking was not wide enough to allow more than one vehicle at a time to use the bridge, and the

Fellow travellers coming from the plateau on to the Indus Plain.

Crossing the Indus River via a pontoon bridge after leaving Dera Ghazi Khan.

speed of each was regulated by a man who walked in front of it carrying two notices in the form of a 'sandwich board'. From behind, the sign on his back read 'This Man Walks To Limit Speed 3 Miles An Hour', and at the end of each pontoon section the bearer did a smart left-turn and saluted, displaying the words 'Thank You' written across his chest.

In between the channels the road was formed by more reeds laid on the sand of the river bed, deposited there by countless spring floods. After some twenty or thirty miles of slow progress, we crossed the Chenab River, which flowed almost parallel with the Indus before joining it a hundred miles further south, and then we left the flood plain and turned north on a tarred road, 'well shaded by acacia trees', towards Multan, the chief city of the Central Punjab.

After passing through Multan, we made a note in the log that we actually ate our lunch in the shade of a tree growing alongside the road, as though we thought that it was an event to be recorded; but that night we camped again on a clay-pan in treeless semi-desert country, much the same as we had seen during the previous five weeks.

Next day the road veered north-east towards Lahore, over the fertile Indus plain, dotted with villages and carrying crops of irrigated cotton and cereals, and again we made a point of remarking that there were 'plenty of trees about'. It seems that we were beginning to realise how much we had missed the sight of them since we had left the Mediterranean, 4000 miles behind us.

Lahore showed many signs of British influence (we stayed at the Elphinstone Hotel in the Mall) and the next morning we called at the office of the Automobile Association of Northern India and were given good information about the route through to Delhi and Agra — the beginning of Kipling's 'Grand Trunk Road'.

The Golden Temple of Amritsar.

Cattle used for drawing water from a well beside the road leading to Delhi.

We left the city by way of the Shalimar Gardens and the 'cantonment', or European quarter, where there were many fine houses and gardens. It was only three hours' drive eastward from Lahore to Amritsar, the principal city of the Sikhs, and about halfway between the two centres we would have crossed the line of the boundary that now divides Pakistan from India.

When we reached Amritsar we had to thread the car through some very narrow streets until we found the Golden Temple, the sacred shrine of the Sikh religion. It was a two-storied building set at the end of a short causeway in the middle of a small artificial lake or 'tank', which was in turn surrounded by other buildings, including a very Gothic-style Christian spire, and which bore the exotic, but quite undeserved, name of the 'Pool of Nectar'.

The roof of the temple itself was decorated with a central dome and Moghul-style 'kiosks', small umbrella-like structures at each corner, all gilded and shining in the sun. The whole atmosphere was tranquil and relaxed — quite unlike that which seems to exist around the Temple in these days of political unrest amongst the Sikhs.

After discarding our shoes we were allowed freely into the Temple itself. The interior of the building was light and airy, with big openings in the marble walls, giving us views out on to the waters of the lake, much as if we were in a boat. In panels spaced along the walls were inlaid designs of birds and fish done with agate, and in alcoves between the windows, a number of handsome Sikh priests, with long combed and curled beards and their hair done up under elegant turbans of different colours, reclined on cushions, reading large and beautifully bound sacred books. They took no special notice of us (I don't remember that there were any other onlookers present) and certainly we were not asked for any money. Nor were we offered a guide, an unusual thing in India around places of interest where sightseers might gather.

A wooden plough pulled by oxen near Ambala.

I do remember feeling slightly embarrassed by being in such close proximity to these apparently holy men, engaged in the pursuit of their religious duties, however uninspiring these might have seemed to us.

Perhaps because of this unease, we were not inclined to stay long in the Temple, but instead allowed ourselves to be picked up outside the precincts by two Sikh civilians and taken to a large walled garden area, where we were shown the bullet marks left on the walls when General Dyer's troops had fired on the crowd in 1935. I don't think that either of us quite understood the significance of the events that our guides were describing, and in any case their English, though certainly fluent enough, was hard to follow. So when they began to ask for what seemed to us to be a large 'contribution for charity' we left them and, with some difficulty, extricated the car from the maze of streets and drove the eighty miles to the *dak* bungalow at Ludhiana.

From Ludhiana we followed the main road south-east past Ambala, through country that was still very dry and without large-scale irrigation, but certainly not permanently arid. There were some big trees along the road in places now, and we began to see groups of small brownish monkeys in them, or on the ground around them. There was dry grass in some of the fields, with grey and white Brahman cattle grazing there.

Cattle were also being used to draw the simple wooden single-furrow ploughs and to pull on the ropes attached to large buckets used to bring water up from wells, whence it was tipped into chutes and drained off to irrigate small areas of crop, or gardens.

Vultures near Delhi.

The vista of a bare 'new' Delhi.

Now we were beginning to leave Moslem India and to enter the country of the Hindus. One indication of this was the obvious reliance on cattle as the predominant form of livestock (as opposed to sheep or goats further to the west and north) and we soon became aware of the respect that was shown to them as semi-sacred animals, which forbade them being killed to eat, or even being castrated, so that every male animal was a bull.

As we drove further east, so did cattle become more common, both in the fields and in the streets of the villages, and it seemed obvious that they were in direct competition with the human population for the available crops, while their return to their owners by way of milk or butter was quite inadequate, mainly because they also lacked sufficient feed.

However, the cattle did make one significant contribution to the welfare of their human competitors. This was to provide them with their main source of fuel in the form of dried dung pats for the cooking fires of the villagers. One result of this was of course that dung was too valuable to be returned to the soil as manure, leading to loss of fertility in the fields.

I made a note in my diary at the time to the effect that official estimates stated that there were then sixty cattle (including buffaloes) in India for every hundred of the human population, a situation that would have represented an enormous burden for an economy where so many people did not have enough to eat.

We were by now not far from the capital Delhi, which may have had something to do with the presence of a large flock of vultures, huge ugly birds and very tame, that we saw either on the ground or perched in low trees quite close to the road, though there was no indication of what had attracted them to that place in such numbers.

At the end of the day we decided to take advantage of the relatively uncrowded countryside to camp out in the open for the last time, finding a patch of short dry grass under some large trees, with a few monkeys running round amongst them.

By 9.30 next morning we were in Connaught Place, the smart shopping centre of New Delhi, the city built twenty or thirty years earlier by the British to be the new capital of the Indian Empire in place of Calcutta. Famous for its spectacular 'vistas', it was then bare of trees and looking rather stark, though flanked by very grand new government buildings. This was said to be the eighth city to have been built at Delhi, or nearby, and we also heard the story of the old prophecy that the rebuilding of Delhi as the capital of India would soon be followed by the ending of British rule there, as indeed happened, just sixteen years after the new city was inaugurated.

After the usual call at the post office, we spent most of the morning at the Red Fort, built in about 1640 as his palace by the Moghul Emperor Shah Jehan, who was also the builder of the Taj Mahal at Agra.

The Moghul rulers of India were of Tartar origin. They had come from the north through Afghanistan under their chieftain Baber in 1526 and had conquered the Punjab, and eventually much of the Indian subcontinent. They ruled for only about 250 years, but in that time were responsible for most of the great buildings for which India is now famous.

The Delhi Fort consisted of a whole series of buildings enclosed in an area of several acres by high walls of red sandstone. The interiors of some of them were splendidly

The new government buildings of New Delhi.

The tomb of the mogul emperor Humayun, near Delhi.

ornamented with intricate stone carvings and inlaid marble panels, particularly the *diwan-i-khas* or 'hall of special audience'. This chamber had contained the famous Peacock Throne, made of solid gold and so named because figures of peacocks, their feathers shining with the colours of inlaid precious stones, stood behind it.

In 1739 the throne was taken to Persia by a later Moghul and partly broken up, though in its present form it is (or was) still to be seen in Teheran. Another treasure of the *diwan-i-khas* was the *koh-i-noor* diamond, now in the British crown jewels.

In the afternoon we saw something of New Delhi, including the Viceroy's House, the Council Chamber (now the Indian Parliament) and the Secretariat. Then we drove the few miles south from the city to Qutab, stopping on the way to see the tomb of the Emperor Humayun, son of Baber and grandfather of Shah Jehan, which monument is believed to have been the model for the Taj Mahal itself.

Qutab is the oldest of the cities of Delhi and its foundation goes back to the twelfth century. Here we stayed as usual at the *dak* bungalow, and in the morning climbed to the top of the Qutab Minar, a tower over 200 feet high, built in the fourteenth century of red sandstone with a circular staircase inside it and decorated on the outside by tiles that spell out inscriptions from the Koran in Arabic lettering.

From the small platform at the top we could look down on the Iron Pillar of Raja Dhava, a solid iron shaft, nearly a foot in diameter, made from forged iron of great purity, which stands in the courtyard below the tower and is believed to date from the seventh century, or even earlier. It is more than twenty feet high, even though it is said that half its length is still below ground. The unsolved mystery, of course, is how so big a shaft could have been forged by hand with the methods of the period.

These involved the reduction of small quantities of iron ore in clay furnaces, heated by charcoal fires, which were blown by simple bellows made from goat skins. The lumps of molten iron obtained from these firings were hammered until welded into larger pieces of solid metal.

We left Qutab in mid-morning and drove the 115 miles south to Agra by four in the afternoon, stopping briefly at Sikandra to look at the tomb of the great Akbar, the son of Humayan and father of Shah Jehan, who, before he died in 1605, had extended the Moghul empire to include most of what is now both India and Pakistan.

My diary describes his tomb as being 'a fine place, with a beautiful marble cenotaph on the 3rd story. From the roof we could see Agra and the Taj' . . . 'On reaching Agra we drove first to the Taj, which looked magnificent as the sun was setting, and is all that one imagined it could be.' I still have a vivid mental picture of how it looked to us that afternoon — its white marble exterior tinged faintly pink with the dust haze of an Indian sunset and the whole building clearly reflected from the pool in the forecourt.

The interior walls, also of white marble, were divided into panels decorated with relief carvings of floral designs, surrounded by intricate mosaic patterns of inlaid semi-precious stones and much of this (as we were told by the guide) was the work of Italian or other European craftsmen imported by Shah Jehan for the purpose. He built the Taj as a mausoleum for himself and his favourite wife, Mumtaz Mahal, who died in 1629, and one authority says that 20,000 men worked for over twenty years to make what must still be the most famous and beautiful building in the world.

At Agra we treated ourselves to the luxury of a night in a good hotel, the Imperial, so

Above: The iron pillar from the top of the Qutab minar.

Top: The minar and iron pillar at Qutab.

as to have a good 'wash and brush-up'; *dak* bungalows not being exactly noted for their bathing facilities. We put on our cleanest clothes, because here we felt that in the company of so many other Europeans (Agra was even then a tourist centre) we must keep up appearances and not 'let the side down' by being too scruffily dressed.

On reflection, I don't think that we ever quite worked out our feelings as regards the British versus Indian situation, which was then becoming a very lively political issue. As Australians, of supposedly democratic instincts, we certainly sympathised with the aspirations of the Indian nationalists for Home Rule, as promoted by Mahatma Ghandi, Nehru, Jinnah and others, and we were sometimes embarrassed by the attitude of aloof superiority shown by certain of the British (often those least entitled to show it) towards the Indian population.

On the other hand we were quite willing to accept the privileges and respect accorded to European holders of British passports and certainly had no intention of mingling too closely with the 'natives', which we had little opportunity of doing anyhow.

In short, we had an each way bet; but we did come to recognise the many benefits, as well as the obvious problems, of a unified British administration over the enormous diversity of races, religions and languages, which still comprise the Indian nation, and which then included the peoples of what are now Pakistan and Bangladesh as well.

Agra had been the great Akbar's capital and, like Delhi, it contained an array of buildings erected by the various Moghul emperors. Apart from the Taj Mahal, the chief of these was the Fort. We went there in the morning after we arrived and my diary reports that 'we beat off the guides, so had a peaceful look round'. The Fort at Agra was perhaps smaller, but certainly no less impressive than the one at Delhi. I recall that there was a most memorable distant view of the Taj across a bend of the River Jumna from the room in the Fort where tradition says that Shah Jehan died.

A view of the Taj Mahal and the Jumna River taken from the Red Fort at Agra.

The red sandstone walls of the moghul fort at Agra.

Inside the fort at Agra.

The Taj Mahal at sunset.

After another visit to the Taj, we left Agra in the late afternoon through streets crowded with people who seemed to be representative of all the many races of India; Agra being in the centre of the northern part of the country, Moslems and Hindus mingled with Sikhs, Jains, Rajputs, Parsees and many others, often unidentifiable as far as we were concerned.

Eventually we got clear of the throng and left the city by way of a bridge over the Jumna, driving south-east again for a couple of hours to the small town of Shikohabad where we stayed for the night.

Next day we passed through the outskirts of Cawnpore and made our first contact with the Ganges, the sacred river of India. The country was still flat, but progressively less arid and the population density increased as we went further east. Villages became more frequent and the roads more crowded, both with pedestrians and the two-wheeled covered carts called *tongas*, each usually drawn by a pair of oxen.

There were not many cars, but small buses and trucks were now quite common and their drivers seemed to progress with one hand almost constantly on the horn button, as they tried to force their way through the crowds in the streets of even quite small villages. Nevertheless, not having much of interest to detain us on the way, we reached Allahabad that night and got a room at the YMCA hostel by way of a change; Allahabad being probably too big a city to be serviced by a *dak* bungalow.

We were now just on 500 miles from Calcutta, with still only a couple of days to spare over the minimum time required for me to catch a train south to Colombo, by way of Madras, to meet up with the P & O liner *Strathnaver*, on which I had booked my passage to Sydney. So we still had the uncomfortable feeling that we were only just on schedule, with almost no spare time to cover unforeseen delays.

At Allahabad, where the Jumna and the Ganges meet, we crossed over on to the northern side of the river by way of a combined road and rail bridge and drove east for seventy miles on a dusty road to Benares (now called by its ancient name of Varanasi). Here we hired a rowing boat with a crew of no less than four men, who rowed us up the Ganges past the various *ghats*, including the burning *ghat*, where they were about to cremate a woman.

Bathing ghats *on the Ganges River at Benares.*

Ghats *on the Ganges River at Benares.*

View of the Benares foreshore from the boat.

The Morris loaded onto a rail truck to cross the Son River.

A *ghat* (pronounced 'gawt') is a level stone landing place with steps leading down into the water. In Benares they are used as bathing platforms from which thousands of Hindu pilgrims enter the sacred river at dawn to wash themselves as part of a rite of religious purification and, when bodies are cremated, the ashes are also thrown into the river.

After this boating excursion we again crossed over the Ganges in the car, this time on a pontoon bridge, and then turned away from it, going south-east on a rough and dusty road to Saseram for the night. When we arrived at the *dak* bungalow there we were disappointed to find that the main leaf of one of the rear springs was broken — the kind of thing that we had hoped to have put behind us when we left Iran. However, long practice stood us in good stead, and we changed over to the spare spring before breadfast, and then drove on a short distance to Dehri, where we had to put the car on a rail truck in order to be able to make use of the only bridge over the wide Son (or 'Sone') River, as it flowed north to join the Ganges.

Later that morning we diverted from the main road to see the Buddhist Great Temple at Budh Gaya. This was an extraordinary looking structure, said to date from the fourteenth century, in a style totally unlike the Moghul tradition of Indian architecture and seeming to consist of a series of heavily ornamented 'layers' of carved stonework, diminishing in size as the building rose higher. It stands on the reputed site of the Buddha's 'Enlightenment' and alongside it there was an ancient-looking peepul tree (which is a kind of fig) revered as a sacred 'Bo-tree', and said to be a descendant of the one under which the actual Enlightenment took place, perhaps in the fifth century BC.

On the inside the Great Temple was, like most Bhuddist temples, rather gaudy and not very remarkable, except for an enormous image of the great Buddha himself, seated in the lotus position. Just the same, our guide was very enthusiastic about it all and extolled the virtues of the 'PWD' (Public Works Department) whose efforts had restored the Temple's structure to its existing good condition.

Back on the Calcutta road (all bitumen by now) the country was assuming a much more tropical look, with wide expanses of paddy fields and groups of palm trees on the ridges. Then we passed through a big area of low hills covered in jungle — 'great tiger country' we were told and we did not doubt the truth of that statement.

We spent that night at the *dak* bungalow at Bagodar, just over 200 miles from Calcutta, with a more optimistic feeling that at last the end of the journey was within our reach.

After Bagodar the country flattened out again and we drove through large areas of rice fields and noted that 'the houses looked more tropical and the people smaller and blacker'. We also passed a large coal-mining and industrial complex around Asansol and pulled-up for lunch near the 100-mile peg from Calcutta, reckoning that we had just crossed the Tropic of Cancer.

Our last night on the road was spent in a small PWD inspection bungalow, about forty miles out of the city, and there we proceeded to clean out the car and sort out our belongings, giving most of our camping gear and any spare rations to the *chowkidar*.

We started out on our last lap in a thick fog that cleared as the sun grew stronger. The road, strangely enough, then became narrow again and wound through thick jungle until we passed through the French concession of Chandanagore, which was almost a suburb of Calcutta.

Just after we crossed the new Willingdon Bridge over the Hoogly River and were about to enter the city proper, by way of an anti-climax, one of the front wheel brakes seized up — the only time on the trip that the braking system had failed us.

Fortunately Ted was able to get the fault repaired without too much difficulty, while I hurried on into town to check with Thomas Cook's about my steamer passage and rail ticket. By mid-day we were able to drive into Dalhousie Square, the city centre, in our own private triumph, quite unnoticed by the crowds of people that filled the main streets of what our little guide-book to India described as 'the second city in the British Empire'.

The Buddhist Great Temple at Budh Gaya.

The date was 14 November — a Monday — and we were, according to the logbook, 80 days and 8255 miles out from London.

It was certainly a great moment for us, but as usual we did not have much time to spend on celebrations. Instead we hastened to find the offices of the Automobile Association of Bengal, where the staff told us about a good boarding house. From this base we set to work to arrange customs clearances and the general paper work necessary for us to be able to sell the car. With this in mind we visited the Morris agents and there found an Anglo-Indian salesman named Abrahams, who expressed some interest in buying our faithful old companion.

That evening he came to our boarding house, and the next morning took the car to be inspected by two Indian mechanics, while at lunch time another one came round to examine it. None of them seemed to notice the plates bolted over the cracks in the chassis, which, though they were solid enough, still had the unfortunate effect of allowing the whole car to sag very slightly in the middle.

In the afternoon of that day (Tuesday) we took a farewell drive in the Morris to see some of the sights of Calcutta. These were mainly in the form of some fine parks and public buildings along the Hoogly River in the centre of the city, laid out and built by the British in the eighteenth and nineteenth centuries, when Calcutta was the administrative and commercial capital of the Indian Empire, with a large European population.

Even so, there were still a few of the privileged Brahman cattle mingling with the traffic in the quieter streets, and at night you could easily fall over a resting cow on your way home, unless you took care to avoid it. The cows seemed to be conscious of their special status and did not seem to feel the need to move for anyone, especially unbelievers.

On Wednesday evening I was due to catch the train south to connect with the ship at Colombo on Sunday, so we had to move fast to finish the negotiations connected with the sale in time to meet that deadline.

Perhaps the relevant page from my diary best summarises the events of the day that saw the end of our expedition:

> Rang Abrahams this morning and went round to his flat.
>
> Finally agreed to sell car for 280 rupees (abt. £21) — we had hoped for Rs 300, or perhaps more, but he would go no higher, in spite of not knowing about the chassis. There was a good deal of delay over registration etc. before the deal was finished at lunch time.
>
> Parted from the old Morris outside the boarding house. After lunch I had to do packing and a bit of shopping.

Howrah Station, Calcutta. The end of a journey.

> Ted went to Cook's and booked by Rangoon, Singapore and Java, also for Darjeeling tonight. He saw me off from Howrah station about 5 pm. — travelled 2nd — not too bad.

It had been a great trip and we both knew that we lucky to have had the chance to do it, but I don't think that either of us was sorry when it was over, our only real regrets being for the things we had not done and the places we had not seen because of being always so short of time.

Concern for the survival of the old car was always a worry, too, but in the end it got us through, in spite of pot holes and corrugations, and moreover the running costs turned out to be surprisingly low.

In the back of the logbook there is a rough list of all our expenses, including payments for the work that was done on the car before we started out, the spare parts we carried, the camping equipment and the tools bought, as well as money spent for food and fuel on the journey.

This last was never itemised, because we took it out of a common 'kitty' and the constant changes of currency made detailed book-keeping too difficult for us to want to even attempt it. The total amount recorded was just over £141 sterling, or about £178 Australian at the then current rate of exchange, and this, we reckoned, was close to being the cost of the steamer fare for two from London to Bombay, at that time.

In my last letter from India, written to my mother, I concluded with, 'Am looking forward very much to getting back. There will be a lot to talk about won't there?'